WHERE'S THE MIRACLE?

Finding Hope Again

STEVE PENNY

DEDICATION

To my wife Marion,
the most courageous and faithful woman I have ever known.
Thanks for being so strong when nothing seemed to make sense.
Thanks for being so true to who we know God called us to be.
Thanks for making the journey so incredibly satisfying.
Thanks for helping me to find faith, hope and love.

IN LOVING MEMORY

To our son Andrew, who always brought us joy.
We value every memory and thank God for the
wonderful times we had together.
We are so proud of you and know that heaven is your true reward.

SPECIAL THANKS

Special thanks to Di Wilson for taking a handful of notes and putting them into some semblance of order. Your input and encouragement has meant so much to us.

Thanks also to Christine Caine for her invaluable help in the final drafts. To both I am very grateful for the love and assistance you have given to us during the project.

Thanks also to our family and friends from around the world who demonstrated true love during our journey through a dark valley. Your friendship helped bring light and make the journey so much easier.

CONTENTS

F O R E W O R D

Bobbie Houston

Sadly we live in a world that is not altogether perfect. As one who believes in a God who is both creator and designer of our lives, I know that His loving intention towards us is total perfection, however we exist in a world where, in many ways, our body, soul and spirit suffer attack. As a race of people, we have refined 21st Century life to quite an art, but this same human race still faces the challenge, the realities, and the tenderness of mortality.

I feel both privileged and humbled to be asked to pen the foreword for this moving and powerful book. My husband Brian and I have known Stephen and Marion Penny for a number of years and consider them amongst our trusted friends. Their ministry and integrity is well respected in this nation and beyond, and most would say that to know them is to smile and love them. In many ways they are your average, down to earth Australian family, who woke up one day and found themselves facing a challenge and seeming tragedy, that no one in their right mind would wish upon another.

I believe this honest story of shock, emotion and courage in the face of extreme adversity, will inspire many. You will find a family rich in love and relationship. You will find a family whose child-like faith questioned and asked why, yet remained undaunted. You will find a family whose natural and spiritual eyes were opened to a world they had never known, yet a world that is a screaming reality for multiplied millions upon the earth, and you will find a family, who emerged triumphant despite the outcome.

I believe this book is heaven breathed. If you are facing a similar challenge, it will enable you to fight this fight of faith and emerge magnificently, and if you are ever called to stand alongside another facing similar circumstances, it will empower you to understand and respond with compassion and faith that is capable of moving mountains.

Yes it is true – sometimes bad things happen to good people, but good people always seem to emerge stronger for the experience. Allow Stephen and Marion Penny, and their family, to walk you through their journey … and together with them, let's all emerge softer, wiser and more compassionate for the experience.

I honour the Penny family for opening their still tender hearts so that others might find strength and blessing, and I honour Andrew Penny for fighting the good fight of faith, which now sees him in the perfect and warm embrace of his Creator and God. The impact of his sojourn on earth will bear fruit and impact many.

Bobbie Houston
Hillsong Church, Sydney, Australia

INTRODUCTION

What do you do when unforeseen circumstances invade your world and turn it upside down?

In 2003 our family went through the worst eight months we could have ever imagined. In just eight short months our eldest son Andrew went from being a healthy, strong six foot one, surf loving young man, to a wasted human shell ravaged by the dreaded disease called cancer; and then on September 4th of that year we watched as our son died before our eyes and there was nothing we could do about it.

Despite all our best efforts at trusting God and keeping our faith strong, we watched as the cancer in Andrew's body came back after each round of chemo to challenge our faith again. We never once gave up on believing for a miracle but at the end of it all our son died and we were left heartbroken and wondering how such a thing could happen.

We wondered how God could allow such a thing and what it really achieved in our lives. We felt as though we had given it our best shot in faith and it hadn't worked.

Since then we have attempted to keep our faith in God strong, and to understand how we can go on trusting God when it seems as though everything we believed for was taken from us. My wife Marion and I have genuinely attempted to keep our faith strong over the years, and so we decided in the early stages of our trial that whatever the outcome, it would not change who we were.

We have also decided since Andrew's death, that we will not allow ourselves to become people who retreat in life because of the apparent "failure" of our faith in God.

Our faith in God did not work the way we wanted it to, and because of this our commitment to live a life of absolute faith was challenged for a period of time, however we went searching for some answers and as usual God is always there for those who seek Him. The answers we have found have been a remarkable help to us as we have endeavoured to go forward in life and live with fresh hope for the future.

I believe I need to write this book, not only for our own healing journey, but for the countless numbers of people who have traveled through the valley of the shadow of death and like us, have come out the other side having lost something or someone very precious. This valley of the shadow of death is the awful time both leading up to, and following a major loss in our lives and is like living under some huge shadow which hangs over us threatening to destroy everything we hold precious.

We traveled through this dark valley and experienced all the dreadful emotions that surface in our trials, finding both the limits of our own human frailty and the overwhelming strength that can only come from a God of supreme love.

We have learnt so much during the time of Andrew's sickness and in the months following his death and I hope that I can relay to you some of the lessons we have learned, and are still learning, as we try to focus on our future.

This is not a book just about our son Andrew, nor the difficult season our family has endured. It is a book about believing when there is nothing else left to do but believe.

About hoping when all hope is gone, and trusting God when all seems lost.

There was a defining moment in this journey when the doctor told us that the chemo was not working and Andrew broke down and cried saying, "where is the miracle, aren't we believing for a miracle?"

These words were to become the challenge which would haunt me after Andrew died. Where was the miracle? There had to be a miracle or my faith was not worth having.

This is the story of how we found our miracle and came to understand more fully God's incredible love for us all.

We pray this will be a book of triumph, about the wonderful works of God and the amazing ways in which he performs His will in our lives, to always help us reach our best and fulfill our destiny in Him.

CHAPTER ONE

ONE PHONE CALL

It all began with the phone call which was to change our lives . . . . forever.

We were in the city of Penrith, on the outskirts of Sydney Australia in February 2003, attending a church conference. Marion had insisted that we should not go, as our son Andrew had been quite unwell with what appeared to be severe back and chest pains. I had stuck to my guns and said we needed to be at the conference, and so we had gone down to Sydney with two other couples from our church ministry team. After attending the conference in the morning, we were having the afternoon off, wandering around the local shopping mall when the dreadful phone call came through. I answered my mobile to hear the most gut-wrenching sound I have ever heard.

It was my twenty-six year old eldest son Andrew, crying and shouting at the same time, "Dad, I've got cancer! Dad, I've got cancer! It's really bad and I have to go to hospital immediately!"

I can't completely explain the feeling that came over me. It felt like fear and dread mixed with shocked disbelief. To make matters worse, I was inside a building where the phone reception was very bad and so Andrew had to repeat everything until we could understand each other. I began to feel panic and helplessness all at the same time.

Awful dread gripped me and I screamed to Marion, "Andrew's got cancer! We have to go home now!"

I told Andrew to go straight to the hospital and we would immediately get on a flight and meet him there. The rest of that day became a blur of activity one can only describe as surreal and chaotic.

On our way to the airport we made many hurried calls to other members of our family, including Andrew's wife Anna, who along with our other two children Luke and Sheree, had already arranged to take Andrew the one hour trip from the Sunshine Coast down to the Royal Brisbane hospital. Within two hours of receiving Andrew's call, we were in the air enduring the worst flight of our lives.

The flight seemed to last forever. We sat in silence not knowing what to say or do, listening to the rhythmic drone of the jet engines outside the window. It all seemed so unreal. My mind kept switching back to the first time we knew there was anything wrong, to now just a month later, with this mad rush of events leading to our son being admitted to hospital with cancer. How could things change so dramatically in just one month?

A month earlier our family had gone to the local golf club for a night out and dinner together. We were having fun; acting crazy like our family always does when they go out to party, when during the night Andrew remarked that his chest was very painful. We just joked that it was a result of his poor golf swing. He thought it was from moving some heavy furniture into his office.

We were in such high spirits that no-one even thought anything of his persistent pain. It seemed like some time since we had been out to a nice restaurant together and we were intent on enjoying it to the full.

In the month following, the pain continued to spread from his chest into his back and became so severe that Andrew would lie awake all night in a hot bath trying to get some relief from the pain. We had no idea his condition had deteriorated to such a degree.

Now with hindsight and knowledge, it is easy to see the symptoms of cancer at work in his body. We should have realised that something was wrong as Andrew had never been one to make a fuss over anything. To see him absolutely wracked with awful pain was disconcerting to say the least. I also said to Marion that it could not just be a back problem as he would not be able to move the way he did. I have had some back problems in earlier years and Andrew's condition did not seem to be the same.

We took him to a number of doctors and to the out-patients casualty area at our local hospital, and each time they gave him some pain killers and inferred that he was perhaps overstating his back problem. We should have known it was more than his back, as his face had begun to turn an awful colour. Andrew had also developed a persistent cough which alarmed one of the ladies working in his office and through her persistence, Andrew finally visited her doctor.

The doctor tapped Andrew's chest and immediately sent him for x-rays, suggesting that something was seriously wrong inside his chest. The x-rays revealed a massive tumor in his chest and it was then that we received the phone call that was to change our lives forever.

It is so true that one phone call can change your life forever, but you never think that it will be your family who will be touched by such unkind events. We always felt like we were somehow invincible and favoured by God, and yet now we were the ones responding to the worst news of our lives.

Our minds were numbed by the suddenness and shock of it all and I felt like screaming at God that this was not the plan that we had agreed upon for our lives. The plan was not supposed to go this way as we believed God had promised us a great future full of His blessings.

We are no strangers to trusting God and believing Him for blessing in our lives. I am the son of a Christian minister who lived his whole life building churches across Australia for God's glory. My parents have given me a genuine ability to believe God for miracles, as we were raised in a miracle environment. My father and mother traveled as evangelists for many years and saw many miraculous healings and miracles during their ministry.

Marion's parents also were committed Christians who served faithfully in their local church all of their lives. Their investment into their local church is a testimony to the grace of God and has been a huge influence in shaping Marion to be willing to step out and have a go for the kingdom of God. Our first attempt at leading a church began when we pioneered a church on the south-side of Brisbane from 1981 to 1991. God blessed us there and we built a wonderful ministry centre as well as planting a dozen other churches out from our church. God gave us awesome miracles during those amazing ten years.

We then felt God leading us to a church in Sydney and ministered there for four years before I resigned to pursue a full time travelling ministry which was to take us across many nations of the world. It was out of this season of world-wide travel that I began to feel as though God was directing us to return to Queensland and build a great church here on the Sunshine Coast.

After having traveled around the world speaking in churches and in conferences non stop for four years, it was wonderful to be settled together as a family in such a beautiful part of the world. We were really enjoying our new found place of ministry and it looked as though all of our children were also finding their futures close to where mum and dad were based.

With Andrew already married, Marion and I were planning the futures of our other children and even dreaming of the sounds of our first grandchildren being heard in the Penny household. Marion and I both began to talk of the joy that grandchildren would bring into our lives. Life was, and was going to be, full of blessing.

Some four years earlier in July 1999 we were given the opportunity to take over a small church on the Sunshine Coast of Queensland Australia. The church, now called KINGS Christian Church, is located one hour north of Brisbane, Australia, in a gorgeous area known for its tropical climate and amazing beaches.

We felt like God had given us every desire of our hearts. In just four years our church had grown from around 150 people to over 1500 people who had acquired property and were looking to build in the near future. Marion and I had also invested in a number of residential properties and had seen the property market boom unbelievably. We had watched as house prices doubled each year making our beachside properties very valuable. We were able to sell some of the properties during this time which gave us a great financial boost during the early years of pioneering the church.

When we took over the church there was very little income and so we decided not to take a salary for the first six months enabling the church to employ a Youth Pastor. This was a great decision as our youth exploded and helped build the church congregation in the early days. We were also able to give quite significantly to the building fund for our new church ministry centre.

Our faith in God was at an all time high and we were seeing some incredible miracles in many areas of our lives. Marion and I had set personal goals to give a significant amount to our church building fund every year. This was to be above our normal giving and therefore we needed to speculate with property to be able to meet our commitments. We took some risks to buy some properties just before the property boom but then realised significant profits to help us with our giving goals. At the time the risks for us seemed very big, but we now realise God was teaching us how to handle finance and wealth for His purposes.

It was to be a great season of personal growth and increase for us and for our church people as they also learnt to trust God for more in their lives. To be honest, we sensed God was preparing us for some great things ahead. We had never really experienced quite this level of blessing before and it seemed to be so easy to achieve. Of course it was through faith in God, but it was also through our risk taking and connections in the property market. God had joined us to some very entrepreneurial people who were out there having a go. We were learning to take risks and to reap the rewards, all for the cause of Christ.

Along with all this incredible blessing, my faith that God was all powerful, all knowing and all present, was at an all time high and I honestly believed God would help us to win in all the things we put our hands to do. Everything we touched seemed to turn to gold; everything seemed perfect. Yet here we were on a flight from Sydney to Brisbane feeling as though we had just been swept up into a huge tidal wave, and we were powerless to do anything about it. Marion and I both just sat silently on the plane with tears streaming down our cheeks.

I could feel the tension rising inside me as we began to approach the Brisbane airport for landing. I knew that I would have to be strong for the rest of the family and tried to take some deep breaths to prepare for the initial shock of seeing our big healthy son now lying in a hospital bed. I just couldn't seem to get my head around it.

We finally touched down in Brisbane and met our second eldest son Luke, who was to drive us to the hospital. Words seemed inadequate as we began to realise that what we thought was a back problem, was so much more serious than the doctors had diagnosed for the entire previous month.

THE JOURNEY OF FAITH

Can Faith Win?

Looking into his eyes so hollow and devoid of life,
And hearing the stetorious breathing of impaired lungs,
It makes one wonder can there be real hope,
And so the battle looms even larger,
And in the back of my mind is the same small doubt,
Can faith win?

I stand at the foot of his bed and watch him
spend another day in the valley of futility,
and with all my strength I take a stand against the insidious
cancer now steadily creeping through his body,
and the procession of bad reports continue,
saying the battle is going against us,
and a knot in my stomach keeps eating away at my strength,
and I wonder,
can faith still win?

Sitting together in a room not big enough
for half as many people,
And pouring over numbers linked to names of blood types,
diseases and other vague treatments,
We listen to learned ones pontificate wisdom from
the classroom of academia,
Yet sharing nothing about the realities of life and death
and the present darkness overwhelming our souls,

And we stop to gasp in air as another bad report is carelessly
dropped upon us,
And we ask with genuine concern,
can faith still win?

The road ahead looks so long and foreboding
in the darkness,
As we turn our car northward for the journey home.
Half asleep and weary from the fight, and not daring to talk
as words can often express the frailty of our humanity,
and in my mind I hear the echo of some inner fear
trying to lift itself into my conscious realm,
and so we glance at each other wondering how we can continue
under such an oppressive cloud,
and I feel like screaming out to anyone who will listen,
Can faith still win?

Gathering together with family and friends of similar spirit
And feeling a strength released just by being together,
I realise that this battle is not to be fought alone,
Nor is it to be an expression of our own
strength and ingenuity,
But rather it is the collective strength of people
who have a common faith in the living God,
who never give up concerning the promises of God and who pray
unceasingly,
and I realise that this is why we continue to fight,
and I boldly declare once again,
Faith always wins!

Steve Penny July 2003

*1 John 5:4, "This is the victory which overcomes,
even our faith."*

When we arrived at the Brisbane airport our son Luke was there to collect us; he informed us that Andrew had finally been admitted to the Royal Brisbane Hospital after a number of hours waiting in the casualty area.

"There are no beds available", was to become a familiar catch-cry over the ensuing months.

We arrived to find Andrew admitted to the oncology ward for leukemia patients. It was a new part of the hospital and looked extremely modern and well equipped. Because most of the people in this ward were seriously ill with a very small chance, naturally speaking, of survival, they assign their best nurses to this ward. We were to thank God many times over for the wonderful caring people who staffed this ward.

Andrew looked awful. Even in the few days we had been away, he had deteriorated badly. Marion and I were shocked to see him in such a state. Doctors had been in to check him out and immediately administered huge doses of morphine to try to alleviate some of the pain. It broke our hearts to see our big healthy fun loving son lying in such agony and pain.

We stayed that night as long as we could and then wandered in a daze out to the car-park to make the hour long trip back home to the Sunshine Coast. I can't remember anything about that first dreadful trip back up to the Coast, except that words were useless.

I do remember in the early days that we began to blame ourselves for not being more aware of Andrew's condition. "If only we had," became a common talking point for some time to come.

The next day presented more shocks and challenges.

Andrew was told that he had germ cell cancer which is very common among teenagers. At 26 years of age, he was at the top end of the age group who suffer from this form of disease. Germ cell cancer usually begins in the testicles in a male, and the ovaries in a female. "This form of cancer treatment is 80% successful", we were assured by one of the medical staff assigned to Andrew.

During that day we met the specialist doctor assigned to Andrew. We were told by all in the ward that we were lucky to have such a brilliant specialist.

He was a nice man who carried the weight of his assignment with some degree of seriousness. However he seemed at a loss to communicate in anything other than the basic facts of the case. When asked a question regarding Andrew's condition he would usually respond with technical terms that left us bewildered and often none the wiser.

This would upset me as it seemed to me as though Andrew was continually referred to as a case study on a piece of paper. He was our son and we were struggling with every human emotion possible, and to see him referred to as just another technical study was more than I could stand.

The first assignment he gave to Andrew was to deliver some sperm for future procreation needs, as the chemo treatment causes infertility and would destroy his ability to produce children. That was a terrible day, as Andrew knew already that he had no ability to issue any sperm. His cancer had for some time been spreading through his chest and back and had made it completely impossible for any physical activity.

When Andrew's wife Anna came into the hospital that day there were many tears. However we were again assured that this form of cancer was 80% curable. Even just hearing this news helped us to believe that we would beat the cancer and win our fight to see our son whole again. However our world would get a lot darker before we were through.

Within the first few days our specialist doctor met with us in the corridor and had a talk. Most of our talks seemed to happen in the corridors for some reason. This first talk shocked us to the core, as he said exactly the opposite to his understudy, who had been assuring us there was some hope.

"This is a very serious case. You must understand that there is little hope of recovery. Andrew's cancer is well advanced and very aggressive."

We were standing out in the corridor by the lifts surrounded by people hurrying to and from their appointments, and we now had to keep control of our fragile emotions as our worst fears were being delivered to us by the very person appointed to be our son's saviour. We had to keep on reminding ourselves that the doctors are not God, and consoled ourselves in that knowledge whenever their reports were less than positive.

From that time on we did not know who or what to believe as we were continually being torn between good and bad reports often delivered on the same day. It was to be a roller coaster of a journey and we would need to hang on with everything we had.

We learnt that Andrew's form of germ cell cancer is not the common form. Usually the primary cancer is in the testicles and it is possible to cut off the testicle and then treat the remaining cancer with various remedies. However Andrew's primary cancer was in his chest as a huge tumor, and it had already spread into his bones. The cancer was also in his spine and he was in danger of his backbone snapping. This form of cancer had a much lower chance of recovery. The eighty percent chance of recovery fell to twenty percent, when they realised where Andrew's primary tumor was located. When this was explained to us we realised that those attending to Andrew did not hold out much hope for his survival. We went home absolutely flat and discouraged when they first told us this very negative report.

And so the tests and treatments began. Andrew's first stay in hospital was to be for five weeks. The doctors decided to administer his first chemo treatment as a mixture called BEP. These letters represented the three poisons that were mixed to form the lethal cocktail called 'chemo'.

Chemotherapy is a mixture of poisons that attack and kill any fast growing cells in the human body. Hair is a fast growing cell therefore it is killed and most patients go bald. Your digestive tract from your mouth to your anus is fast growing and therefore comes under attack. This causes ulceration of the mouth and digestive tract etc. causing sickness and an inability to eat and retain food. Cancer is also a very fast growing cell and therefore is also attacked by the 'chemo'.

Everyone responds differently to chemo, and there are varying mixtures and dosage strengths. Andrew was on the strongest legal dose possible. We had talked with Andrew as to whether he wanted to have the chemo treatments and he had decided he would try all available medical treatments as well as trusting God for complete healing. These two stances did not seem to us to be out of character with faith and so we agreed that we should do everything possible. Andrew's body responded dreadfully, and from day one he was unable to keep anything down. He tried everything and so did we. Marion would cook him all kinds of things, and I would be sent over to the service station across the road from the hospital to get some little thing he fancied. All to no avail, as it would come up again within just minutes. The vomiting became so painful for Andrew that he began to dread even trying to eat, and many an argument was had with a concerned mum encouraging him to try again. After the brief moment of pleasure and indulgence, the pain would return and the vomiting started all over again. This never improved during the whole time of Andrew's sickness.

As a parent you feel absolutely helpless watching your child deteriorate before your eyes. It was soon to become apparent to me that the senior specialist who was a male and his female understudy were playing 'good cop – bad cop' with us. The understudy was a wonderful lady who became quite close to Marion and was always so optimistic and concerned. Her bedside manner was so uplifting and encouraging and her reports were always offering some degree of hope – 'good cop'. However when the senior specialist came in with his entourage of assistants, the understudy would remain silent as he unloaded his pessimism in a most matter of fact and technical way – 'bad cop'. He wasn't a worse person, he gave us what he felt we needed to know, but we just didn't want to hear it. We desperately believed for a better outcome.

Looking back I believe he knew from the outset that the cancer was aggressively progressing and that it would take a miracle to change its course. That's where we came in. We believed in miracles. We were Christians and God would undertake for us. We were so optimistic and confident that our faith would produce a miracle to the glory of God. After all we had already had a major attack of cancer in Marion's body and God had healed her.

Just a few years after we were married Marion was referred by her doctor to a cancer specialist because of some lumps in her breast. As soon as the specialist examined her he arranged for Marion to be admitted to hospital for a biopsy and if his prognosis was correct, a mastectomy.

The specialist who was highly respected, was adamant that the mastectomy operation would be required and told his theatre nursing team to prepare for the full operation. We did what we knew to do. We went to prayer and got our church and friends praying and believing for a miracle.

I will never forget the bewildered look on the surgeons face when he came out of the operating theatre to declare that everything was clear. His comment was, "you never can trust those damn x-rays." The lumps were benign and posed no threat whatsoever. He had been so certain that it was a malignant tumor. We knew God had performed a miracle then, and we believed He would do it again in our son Andrew's case.

Day after day dragged on and our lives began to take on a bizarre routine. We agreed with Andrew's wife Anna that it was best that she keep working as a graphic design artist, and that Marion and I would go down each day to be with Andrew. Anna would get time off whenever she could and then spend the weekends at the hospital. I felt as though Anna needed to stay employed so that when Andrew came home they would have some employment to keep them financially afloat. We decided to close Andrew's graphic design business after a few months as he had decided that he wanted to serve God in a different way when he was well again.

> *I tried not to focus on the badness of our circumstance, but on the goodness of our God.*

And so we began to form a routine that was to continue for the next seven months. I would get up between four and five in the morning to spend time with the Lord - praying and worshipping God for His goodness in our lives. I tried not to focus on the badness of our circumstance, but on the goodness of our God.

I would sit in a chair in the lounge of our rented property looking out the front window waiting for the first rays of the rising sun to announce that a new day of hope had arrived. I had such an assurance those mornings that the Lord would do a miracle that most of the time I was quite calm and relaxed before God. I would remind Him of all His promises, thanking Him that He was able to do abundantly more than I could ever ask or even think to ask for.

During the day however it was often a different case. When faced with Andrew's declining condition, we would be besieged with doubts and all kinds of feelings, but in those early hours of the morning, my sanity and soul would be restored and strengthened by my loving heavenly Father.

When Andrew came home for a few days between treatments, he would sometimes get up and sit with me in the lounge. Rugged up with blankets, sheepskin boots and knitted woollen hats (beanies), we sat there like two old men, often silent yet enjoying each others company.

Because Andrew's cancer had spread into his bones and lower back it became very difficult for him to walk from quite early on. He was also very weak from lack of nourishment due to continual vomiting. This bothered the doctors as they worried about loss of function in Andrew's legs, and so they would often cajole him into doing a lap of the hospital ward. This usually ended with Andrew vomiting and flopping back onto his bed exhausted. We decided not to harass him into doing anything unless he wanted to.

The times at home during Andrew's sickness have become very special memories to us. Andrew had always been a good son to us and we have an amazing treasure of precious memories from his life, but the memories of those few weeks at home have somehow stuck with us as special snapshots of his faith and courage in action.

One such memory is of our trips in the car to check out the surf. Andrew loved surfing and so when he felt well enough for a little ride we would help him into the car and then quietly check out his favourite surfing spots. We would also check out the progress on our new house as construction had started during this time.

When Andrew was in hospital, I would go to the church office for the morning and return home around mid-day to pick up Marion to make the daily trip down to the hospital. Sometimes Marion would have left earlier, feeling the need to be there and spend as much time with Andrew as possible. We would then stay at the hospital until around eight at night.

The trips home became an ordeal as we began to experience fatigue, and so we would share the driving. Some nights it was impossible for me to drive and so I would sleep on the back seat while Marion battled on.

We would arrive home so exhausted and spent, but thankfully find a fully cooked meal waiting for us every night. One of our young ministry team couples had taken it upon themselves to arrange people to prepare the night meal for us.

However one night, on reaching home after a very difficult day, I was really looking forward to eating and then off to bed. This was the one night that the team did not bring a meal. We are so grateful for the team's generosity to have made us meals – it was beyond expected – but on this night, it was the straw that broke me.

Marion simply stated that she was content with a piece of toast. I reacted badly and stormed out of the house to go and satisfy my body with a good feed of Kentucky Fried Chicken.

Once I had eaten to my full, I sheepishly returned home to try to make amends for my outburst.

Marion as usual overlooked my reaction, and again we realised how important it is to keep our relationship strong. We must support each other. We often found ourselves stretched to the limit and even little things, at times caused us to react poorly.

There were many moments when not only our faith was being stretched to the limit but so was our relationship. We had moments when we needed each other so desperately to draw strength from one another, and then there were other times when we needed a little extra space just to breathe our own air and deal with our fragile emotions. Sometimes it just takes a little time to get our attitudes right and then come out smiling to face the battle once again. We certainly learnt some things about our relationship during our journey of faith.

> *We learnt – that there is nothing stronger than encouragement from the partner God has given you in life.*

We learnt - that we must never blame each other for things, and to quickly put things right when one of us (usually me) was acting badly.

We learnt – that we are not perfect and we need to give each other room to deal with difficult situations in our own way.

We learnt – that there is nothing stronger than encouragement from the partner God has given you in life.

We learnt – that one of us could be strong one day and the other the next, and that the strong one needed to help the weaker one.

We learnt – never to give up or allow the other partner to give up. We were a team and together we could come through this challenge.

We learnt – that each partner needed contact with their own friends to maintain some form of normal contact with the real world.

Many people suggested that we drop out of church leadership during this period, and to be honest, it would have been so easy to do just that. However I felt like I needed to stay connected to our church as we drew such strength from these wonderful people who supported us in amazing ways during this time.

> *We learnt the power of our relational networks and that church is much more than a weekly meeting of strangers.*

That was the smartest thing we did during the whole ordeal. The people of our church were absolutely amazing. They loved us when we needed some loving and forgave us when we didn't always act right; and they especially carried us in prayer through our whole journey of faith. It was a journey that would have been a nightmare without these loving gracious people.

Many of our people in their desire to encourage us sent special words from the Lord about Andrew's total healing. I received every one of them with absolute joy.

We were all believing together for a miracle. We learnt the power of our relational networks and that church is much more than a weekly meeting of strangers. We were connected with real people who walked this journey of faith with us and we found strength in knowing they were there for us.

> *You don't have to be the great miracle worker, just be there and offer normal friendship and support.*

Other people however avoided us throughout the whole experience. Usually with the excuse, "I just don't know what to say." I can fully understand how they felt, as I have often felt useless and at a complete loss as to what to say when confronted with the tragic circumstances others have had to endure. But it was hard to understand as some people who had been quite close, seemed to avoid us during our ordeal.

If you have someone near you who is suffering in some way, then please make contact with them as often as you can. Just provide them with normal human contact. You don't have to be the great miracle worker, just be there and offer normal friendship and support. It means so much to people going through a dark valley. They don't expect you to know where to go or what to do; they just want to know that you are there with them. Just ask for permission to call and then tell them that you 'don't really know what to say', but wanted to let them know that you are always thinking about them and are there for them should they want some company.

I thank God for the ladies in our church who took Marion out for a coffee. It always made such a difference. During this time our family and friends often came into the hospital to spend time with us as Andrew was usually bombed out with drugs for longs periods of time. These coffee times with family and friends became moments of normality, even for just a few minutes, as we grappled to keep our heads above water in the foaming sea of insane circumstances.

> *We also realised we had to make choices during the journey that would affect us and our future forever.*

This journey of faith – as we called it; seemed to stretch on far past the time frame that I had allocated to it in my mind.

I had personally given God three months during the first "chemo" treatment to add His touch and heal Andrew of cancer. As the months continued and the treatments increased, I realised that this was not going to be a one off miracle event, but a journey. We needed to change our attitude to see that God in His wisdom was taking us somewhere. We would end up in a different place from where we began. This "journey of faith" was not just about Andrew's miracle, but had become a journey that we would all have to complete and come through. We would all need our own faith and each one would emerge from this valley of darkness with a unique story to tell.

This journey of faith helped us to see that life is a journey of learning and that we never stop learning new things as we progress and grow in this classroom of life.

We also realised we had to make choices during the journey that would affect us and our future forever. We could never be the same again after this journey of faith. The Bible Psalmist declared, *"Yea though I walk through the valley of the shadow of death, I will fear no evil, for thou art with me."* *(Psalm 23:4)*

As time went on it became apparent that this journey of faith could possibly lead us to walk through the valley of the shadow of death, and we needed to adjust our thinking and faith to complete the journey and come through the other side as better people. However I just couldn't or wouldn't accept such a scenario that Andrew may die, and found it a real challenge as Andrew's condition deteriorated and the shadows of this valley of death began to deepen around us on every side.

Thankfully God was with us, and even though the shadows lengthened and the darkness increased we knew that there was a light within us that could dispel the darkness and keep it from invading our soul.

The light of our faith kept us strong during some of the darkest hours I have ever experienced in my life. This really was to be our "journey of faith."

CHAPTER THREE

THE THINGS I REMEMBER
A MOTHER'S PERSPECTIVE

Marion was born to help others, and when Andrew became sick she just rose up and became an absolute angel of mercy and care. Not once during the whole time did she ever want time out and resolutely continued to tend to Andrew's needs whenever she could.

Marion's story is amazing and so I will let her tell it as she remembers it.

The things I remember . . . I must say that the memories of those months are for the most part not happy ones – there were a lot more tears than there were laughs – however our emotions are our emotions and tears are just as real as smiles.

I remember that I cried a lot. I remember one of the nurses saying "Off you go to the cafeteria and get lots of frothy coffee – frothy coffee, that's what you need!"

February 2003 was a month of Andrew not feeling well, being in a lot of pain, and nobody – the doctor, the physiotherapist, the hospital – nobody having a clue. I say the doctor, because he was not Andrew's doctor – Andrew had never HAD a doctor – he had never been sick. He was a big healthy basketball playing, surfboarding 6'1" young man of 26 years.

I remember the night at the end of January 2003 when Steve and I took Andrew and Anna out for dinner. We all had a good time, laughing, eating too much – except for Andrew who said he had a pain in his chest and couldn't eat his steak – not like him!

I remember that for the next couple of weeks Andrew would say "My chest isn't right – Anna can hear it gurgling. And my back is so sore I have to get up in the night and have a really hot bath to get relief from it. Also I'm sweating so much, the doona is saturated." We couldn't figure out what could be wrong.

I remember the day Andrew rang me and said "Mum can you take me to the hospital – I can't stand this pain in my back." I remember waiting ages in the emergency waiting room and then when they took him inside, waiting again until they gave him a pethadine shot in the leg and saying "Off you go!" They think young blokes with back pain are trying to get out of work!

I remember taking him to the physiotherapist – and afterwards, as he painfully tried to get into the car him saying "I just want to die – Anna would be better off anyway – I've got insurance." And I remember my response (now with regret) "Well, you're NOT going to die, so you've just got to get some weight off and get this back sorted out!" (The cancer had spread from the tumor the size of a grapefruit in his chest to his back – we had no idea!)

I remember the Sunday afternoon he came to our house to get his hair cut by our hairdresser friend. She was colouring mine and he waited a little while. Then, and with a look I will never forget, he said, "I have to go home." His face was almost orange and the look was haunted. Our friend was to say to me later when we knew what he had, "Marion, I'll never forget that look." I will never forget it either.

I remember taking him to the local doctor. He wrote him a prescription for what he called "pretty strong pain killers". I collected them from the chemist and she said, "The doctor has prescribed two of these, but they're pretty strong. I recommend taking one first to see if he really needs two." The next morning Andrew's report was, "Those two painkillers did nothing!!" My stomach turned over. I felt so helpless and nobody seemed to know anything.

I remember the Monday morning we were to leave for a conference in Sydney. I was concerned about Andrew and rang to see how he was. "I'm no good Mum – my chest is rattling and my back is no good." Andrew always understated – he never complained.

I remember not wanting to go to conference – but what could I do – we just thought his back was "out". Steve had put his back out on occasions and it was always painful – that's what we thought it was.

I remember a friend from church saying to me "Marion, I don't like the look of Andrew. Do you think he'd mind if I made an appointment with my doctor for him?" She did that and while we were in Sydney, she picked him up and took him to her doctor. We had tried to get in to see other doctors, but the response each time was, "Sorry we aren't taking any new patients."

I remember we were in a shopping centre in Sydney when Steve's mobile rang.

I remember hearing Steve say "Hang on mate, I can't hear you." Then, "Ok, mate, we'll be on the next plane home."

I remember saying "He's got leukemia, hasn't he?" I have no idea why I said that – it was my first thought – probably because of the colour he had become. Steve said, "No, he has a tumor the size of a grapefruit in his chest."

Later, in the course of his illness, Andrew confided, "That was a hard phone call to make!"

I remember waiting in the airport for a plane. I remember ringing my mum to tell her and she said, "It's probably not malignant." I hadn't even thought of that.

Thank God for her positive outlook on life. She always believed until the day she died that Andrew would recover beautifully. I thank God she didn't live to see Andrew die.

My mother died three months after Andrew was diagnosed.

I remember when my friend's doctor saw Andrew he immediately ordered urgent x-rays. As soon as the x-rays were in his hand, he said to Andrew, "Get your wife here and any of your family you can. I want you in the Brisbane hospital this afternoon." The Brisbane hospital is an hour and a half from the Sunshine Coast where we live. So while we flew from Sydney to Brisbane, Luke, our other son, Sheree our daughter, and Anna, Andrew's wife, drove Andrew to the hospital. The doctor could have referred Andrew to a hospital in our area but he said he would have to wait three to four days to see a consultant and he didn't have three or four days. His fear was that Andrew could become a paraplegic at any moment because of the tumor's proximity to Andrew's spinal cord.

I remember that even though it was all meant to be arranged, Luke, Anna, Sheree and poor, very sick and in pain Andrew, walked all over the hospital trying to find out where Andrew was "expected"! Luke finally became very exasperated and then some "action" happened, resulting is a bed being found for Andrew in Oncology. That's where we found him after getting off the plane from Sydney.

I remember being very shaky – I think it was shock. That's where he remained for the next five weeks straight.

I remember the day he had lots of tests – he had already been in hospital for four days! He was on a hard stretcher in unbearable pain for most of the day while they conducted numerous unpleasant tests.

I remember that night standing at the foot of his bed and massaging his legs as high up as a mother can decently go because he was in agony.

I remember the young male trainee doctor coming in and saying "I'll be back in a minute mate with morphine." I remember the relief we felt when the morphine kicked in.

I remember a nurse thinking I was such a fabulous person because I said to her one day that I was grateful we lived in a country where we had morphine at our disposal! That's something to get recognition for!

I remember the Monday morning chemo was scheduled to start (five days after being admitted to hospital). Because chemo can totally wipe out sperm production forever, they wanted Andrew to be taken to the sperm bank where a donation can be obtained for the future so he and Anna could have their own children. Andrew's doctor flatly refused to let him be taken anywhere – he said, "You aren't going anywhere – you are far too sick." I remember Andrew crying, saying, "Anna will be so upset." I remember all of us crying and one of the nurses saying, "You'll have me crying in a minute." She already was! She said, "Don't worry – I've seen babies come out of these oncology wards" You always remember the nice ones – they make the whole ordeal that much easier. I know they feel embarrassed to cry, but I always loved them all the more, because it was like they cared enough to cry!

I used to try to go out of Andrew's room if I got upset, but he said to me one day early in the journey, "Mum, don't worry if you cry – I don't mind, you don't have to go outside." He was always thinking of other people.

I remember when someone said to me after he died, "Now you have to get over all the awful things Andrew said when he was sick." I replied, "He never did. He never said anything awful to us." That's a blessing, and a lesson I hope I've learned if ever I get really sick.

I remember the night we took Steve's computer to the hospital and Sheree was showing Andrew all the happy Christmas photos. We were all smiling and then I noticed Andrew's stomach beginning to heave and the tears well up in his eyes.

He said, "I miss my life." We all cried.

I remember on about day 12 of chemo his hair beginning to fall out. That was never a big deal really, because our boys were often shaving their heads or getting number one clippers.

I remember that Andrew's body would not bounce back after the chemo. He vomited constantly and his platelet count would not come back up. We were such novices to all this – now we realise it was because his bone marrow was affected by the cancer. Sometimes ignorance is bliss.

I remember the day the doctor said, "We've got to get you out of here Andrew. You've been here five weeks. If the senior oncologist says ok, you can go today."

Andrew and I prayed urgently that he would be able to come home. The senior oncologist (known by the younger oncologists as number one God) came in, looked at the figures (cancer is all about figures on paper!) and gave the okay. I cried, Andrew cried and his female oncologist cried.

I remember as we drove out of the hospital, Andrew burst into tears and said, "I just never want to come back here." That was out of the question as he had only had two lots of the four BEP (a concoction of chemo drugs known by their initials) that they said would "do the trick." These four lots plus three more of a different concoction were still to come, and none of them did the trick.

Then began the daily drive to Brisbane to have chemo administered, blood transfusions, platelet transfusions, morphine shots, phenergan drips to counteract the affects of platelet transfusions (the body can reject them) and an endless, monotonous array of never pleasant tests.

I remember that, unlike other people who were made to sit for hours in the waiting rooms we were always seen to immediately. Andrew always walked in with a red ice-cream container under his chin as he was always close to vomiting, and they always said "come straight in", and always found a bed for him. We were so very grateful for that.

I remember the day one of the nurses decided this wasn't to her liking and so she said, "from now on you have to have an appointment and how would it be if everyone did this and just expected the doctor to be called!" Thankfully it never happened – the doctor always came and found Andrew. They liked him – he always co-operated and never complained. I must admit that in the Day Oncology Ward, I didn't see many other people as sick as Andrew.

I remember the day he was being plugged in for more chemo and while the nurse was plugging him in she had her shoulder under his back propping him up so he could vomit once again. I noticed she had tears in her eyes and I had to turn my head and try to regain my composure. When I say "plugging him in", - he had a catheter put into his chest which went up by his collar bone and down near his heart – it sounds terrible, but it was marvellous. It was called a Hickmans catheter. It had many "double adapters" hanging out of his chest, and many drugs could be administered at once. Blood could be transfused etc. instead of having to have a needle inserted into a vein – veins collapse with chemo, so that becomes an awful prospect.

I remember five days after we brought him home from hospital after his first five week continuous stay (he was to have a few of these long stays during the course of the disease) we were having to take his temperature three times a day because if there was an infection of any kind, we had to rush him back to the hospital. About three in the afternoon, Andrew's temperature began to climb. We rang the oncologist. She said, "bring him straight down." Then another nightmare begins of just waiting and waiting for hours in the Emergency Admissions area. You can go into Emergency okay, but then there are no beds available! They tell you, "Sorry, we don't have any beds in oncology. We don't know when there will be one available." They sent an Oncology nurse down to Emergency to administer the antibiotic through the Hickmans because of the danger of infection when chemo has wiped out the immune system. About this time, Steve went across the road to get a bottle of water. While he was outside they found Andrew a bed in the Ear Nose & Throat Ward! One of the girls on Emergency Admissions rang her cousin who is in our church and told her, "The Pennys are here with Andrew and we have no beds. She was quite distraught. Her cousin told her what to do in no uncertain terms –"Pray, Natasha, PRAY!" The bed was okay, but it certainly wasn't in an Oncology Ward where they knew what to do with him. I cried all the way home! Or at least half way! I felt so desperate leaving him there but there was no choice.

I remember the first time I had to clean the Hickmans catheter. It had to be kept sterilised. An absolutely sterile atmosphere is desirable as much as possible because of the destroyed immune system. Infection is very dangerous and can be fatal. Hand-washing is done on the way into the hospital and on the way out and many times in between.

I am no nurse and so cleaning this thing, all the while fearing not doing it properly and hurting Andrew, caused my hands to shake. Andrew was a tower of strength, saying, "Come on mum, you can't be any worse than those nurses." It seemed to me that the weaker Andrew became physically, the stronger he got emotionally and spiritually.

I remember that the Hickmans had to be cleaned after Andrew's shower. He would have a shower, manage to put on his undies, and literally flop on the bed and call for me to come "do the Hickmans".

I remember the day he didn't make it to the bed. Anna called out "Marion, something's wrong." Andrew had got out of the shower and collapsed into a chair. We pulled a mattress onto the bathroom floor and the two of us got him down on to that so he could get some blood back into his head. He was the colour of the sheets! He stayed there until Steve got home and could help him up onto the bed.

I remember another day when he collapsed in the hospital shower. I didn't care who thought what of me. I yelled from the doorway for "Help!" I never knew there were so many people in earshot! Doctors, nurses, came from everywhere.

I remember him trying to eat. He could never stomach hospital food so we thought it would be better when we got him home. The first five weeks in hospital he "survived" on green cordial. We figured it wasn't a matter of life and death because he was carrying extra weight on him when he went into hospital. When he came home after these five weeks in hospital every morning he would ask for eggs on toast – and so whatever he felt like eating, was what I would make. We would make sure he took the anti-nausea drugs prior to

> We have
> angels all
> around us.
> Sometimes
> we just
> don't see
> their wings.

eating. They were meant to alleviate nausea but never did. We had every nausea drug known to man – might as well have had a drink of water!

The eggs would go down alright, but no more than 15 minutes later (sometimes less), he would vomit explosively! I remember one morning, he had just spewed up everything, and he said "Let's try again, Mum." So we did. It was a wonderful day if ever he kept food down for 2 hours. I figured surely his body was getting something. However, I did notice on a report his oncologist wrote, that he was suffering from severe anorexia!

I remember one day after he had vomited yet again he cried and said "I'm starving." He literally was starving to death. It broke my heart. From the time your baby is born, your job is to make sure he eats. It's a mother's job!

There were people who we will never forget – practical people who could see what needed doing, and did it. One of the young mothers in our church got a roster going and every night there was a meal cooked for us! We were so grateful. She lived 15 minutes from us – would have the cooked meals delivered to her house each night, then bring them to our house. Our house was never locked, so she would come in, deliver the meal, take away any dishes from the night before and repeat the process every night for the next six months. Our gratitude to her and all the ladies in our church who so graciously cooked can never be measured.

I had another friend who said to me "Whenever you're at the hospital and Andrew falls asleep, ring me. I'll drop everything, be there in 15 minutes and take you for a coffee." We have angels all around us. Sometimes we just don't see their wings.

One other young couple in our church put one thousand dollars in Andrew and Anna's letterbox every month. Could they afford it – probably not! Angels without wings!

Other people sent us money – If ever you know someone who is sick, and you have no idea what to do – send money!! When someone is sick, the income goes down and the expenses soar – hospital food, hospital parking, medicines etc. I was telling the social worker at the hospital how one of our young friends had helped Andrew and Anna out by putting $500 in an envelope for them. Her response astounded me. She just smiled and said, "Who in her family has been sick?"

I remember the doctor's phone call after the four lots of BEP had been done. She said "I'm sorry Mrs. Penny, we haven't got it all. We can probably do some other chemo, but the chances are going down." We all cried.

One of the numbers that is used in Andrew's type of cancer is called the AFP. The lower it is the better – it should be below 5, preferably 0. When Andrew was diagnosed, his was 3000. With each dose of chemo, the AFP should drop and continue to drop. Andrew's AFP would always drop, but before the next chemo could start, it would once again raise its ugly head. I began to visualise it as a snake in his body – one that needed to be dragged out and killed!

I remember that if the AFP went down, his doctor would hurry up to the ward and say, "Good news, Andrew, the AFP is down." But if the AFP had been tested that day and we didn't see the doctor, I would know it had gone up again. They were horrible days.

I remember after the four BEP, Andrew went into hospital again for the next lot of chemo. This lot was so lethal that he had to be in hospital so they could keep him under constant watch. I went into the hospital about midday and Andrew said in a voice I will never forget – flat and just matter of fact – "The AFP is 1600." You could have scraped me up off the floor and my chin imprint is still in 5C bed 7! That was extremely bad news!

I remember the day the nurses came and said "We are moving you out of this single room today Andrew, we have someone very sick coming in!" If you ever want to feel powerless this is it. So they moved him into a double room with a man who would not turn his TV down. He would fall asleep at night with it on very loudly and Andrew could not get any sleep. I remember not wanting to go home at night and leave my boy there! All I could do was pray every night and ask God to send his angels. That angel came in the form of a nurse who realised what was happening and moved him to a different room with a nicer roommate. Who wants roommates at all when you are so sick, but there is no choice. The next roommate was fairly quiet, but when his family came to visit, all they talked about was the next tattoo they were getting. We realised that like us, they too were just trying to talk about life and not dwell on all the details of the sickness.

I remember the day Andrew wanted us to take him back to his and Anna's unit by the beach. He staggered along, hanging on to Steve's shoulder for support, managed to get up the few stairs, into the unit where his brand new surfboard was still standing against the wall. He had bought it just before be began to get sick. It was his vow to get better and ride it. I realised he wanted to go back because he had been happy there and was trying to regain his happy life. We ordered pizza from the restaurant downstairs. Andrew managed to eat one piece and promptly vomited. I don't think we went back there again.

Andrew and Anna had moved in with us when he came home from hospital. Anna was working full time as a graphic designer and even though she would have gladly given up work to look after and be with Andrew, Steve thought it better she stay at work "because when Andrew gets better, he won't be able to work for a while, and you'll need an income." Hindsight is a wonderful thing!

I remember the night I sat bolt upright in bed, woke Steve up and said "I know why they aren't giving us the results (they had promised us results of tests and kept stalling). The treatment isn't working!" Steve told me I was being ridiculous. But it turned out to be the case that the treatment was not working.

I remember thinking these doctors were heartless, sometimes not telling you things, and sometimes not saying goodbye when you left the hospital – but I realise now that they are human – and they can't trust their own emotions when they really like a patient and it isn't working out. Andrew's doctor said to me one day with tears in her eyes, "Life sucks sometimes."

I remember one morning ringing Andrew in the hospital and him telling me he had fallen during the night and couldn't get up. He had stood up to use his urine bottle, put the bottle in its cradle hanging on the edge of the bed, and fallen to his knees, where he remained for 10 minutes or so until a nurse had time to answer his bell. I remember telling my brother Tom and his response was "Oh, the poor kid." I cried.

I remember three months after Andrew was diagnosed getting a call in the middle of the night and it was my brother saying, "Marion, I've got bad news – Mum has just passed away." She lived in the same street as my brother. At 1 a.m. she had called him and said, "Come and bring your key." She obviously knew she wouldn't be able to get up and answer the door. She was dead when he got there 5 minutes later. It was such a shock. I had seen her that day and every day before that – we were very close. Andrew staggered out of bed and when he heard the news, he cried and said "She has died because you're so busy looking after me, you haven't had time to look after her." I remember my reply – "No, Andrew, I have been praying that when it's Ma's time to go that God would take her in her sleep and he has answered my prayer." He seemed to cope with that but I knew he was heartbroken.

My mum's funeral took place on the Sunshine Coast but she had wanted to be buried near my father's graveside in Brisbane which was an hour away. I went to the funeral but made a decision I would not be attending the graveside, because Andrew was too sick. When your child is sick, decisions that would otherwise be inconceivable become commonsense.

People say, "How did you cope?" I would say my faith in God was the biggest thing that kept me sane. I have faith in the fact that God is in control – even if I didn't like what was happening. I believe we don't know everything and God does! Simple – but I can't explain it any other way. Do I still trust God? Yes. We miss Andrew terribly, terribly, terribly, but we know he is in heaven and one day we will see him again, and my mother and my father and my friends' children (several of them) who have also gone there before us.

> *I would say my faith in God was the biggest thing that kept me sane*

I remember the day the doctor came into Andrew's room and said "Well Andrew, we are not going to beat this disease." We were all very emotionless. I think about that now and I can't

-42-

imagine that we didn't cry – but we didn't. And Andrew just said, "We'll just have to wait and see." He also had a faith in God and believed up until the very last God would heal him. God has healed him – it just wasn't on this earth – but now in heaven he is happy and healed. Was it the outcome we would have chosen? Never! But we do trust that Almighty God is in control. Have we cried buckets – tons of them!

I remember the day Andrew's walking changed from straight legged walking to grasshopper legs – bent and no strength. The next day at the hospital he said to the doctor "I'm a bit worried about my legs – they're so weak." The doctor put his hand under Andrew's foot and said "Press – Andrew, press." "That's as hard as I can do it," said Andrew. Immediate MRI. The tumor was pressing on the spinal cord and now it was going to stop him having any strength in his legs – not able to stand or walk.

A nurse came over at this point and said "Andrew, can you come over to this bed please?"

Steve said in a voice with an edge to it "He's not going anywhere till I lift him there!"

She was the loveliest nurse, and knew us well, and had not realised this latest setback, but did not for one split second show any annoyance at Steve's snappiness. I remember her response, "I'm terribly sorry Steve, I had no idea." Anyone who tells you that tragedy or stress turns you into a saint, has never been in tragedy or stress. From my perception stress like that turns you into people who are just managing to hold it together, and not always succeeding.

I remember that the doctor ordered five doses of radiation to try to shrink the tumor back off the spinal cord. So the nightmare intensified. Steve now had to lift Andrew into a wheelchair, into the car, out of the car, onto the radiation table face down, etc. etc. Andrew was a tall boy of 6ft who by now was pretty much skin and bone, but to lift such a tall person with no leg function at all in and out of the car was no mean feat. I began to worry that Steve would be the next one with back trouble.

I remember the day I talked with the Palliative Care doctor at the hospital and told him that when we get Andrew home we were going to get him tube fed through the Hickmans to try to get him some strength back. I will never forget his words, "Oh don't do that Mrs. Penny, Andrew's body is shutting down. You will just confuse everything if you do that." I was stunned.

He said, "Do you think Andrew realises it is so close (he predicted "weeks")?" I said I wanted him to go speak to Andrew on his own so that Andrew could ask him any questions he wanted to without me there. He came back to me and said "Andrew realises – he is trying to protect you guys."

I spoke to his female oncologist, and told her what he had said. Her eyes welled up with tears and she said "Will you let me know when please, Mrs. Penny." I think that's when it became more real. We both cried – she wiping her eyes and saying "Oh God! It's so unprofessional for doctors to cry!" – but doctors are human and caring, most of them and they had become like family to us.

I remember the day Andrew looked at me with tears running down his cheeks and said "I can't leave Anna." He knew he was dying and was so worried about Anna. I just said "We'll look after Anna." Anna was 23 at the time. She lived with us for the year following Andrew's death until she was able to move into her own house. We love Anna as we love our own Luke and Sheree.

The palliative care doctor was correct. Andrew died 9 days after his prediction of "weeks" at home, with all of us around his bed. Anna had spent the whole previous day with him, Sheree had spent much of the previous night sitting on his bed, and Luke had spent time with him before going to work that morning.

At 7.45 a.m. Steve and I were in the room and his breathing changed. We looked at each other and we knew. At 8.15 he breathed his last. We were heartbroken – he was such a fun person – made us laugh – and we miss him. When people go out of your life, it leaves a big hole! There is comfort in knowing we will see him and all the others who have gone before us – we don't grieve as those who have no hope as the Bible says – but loving the ones we still have with us becomes more important. When people pass out of our life, we will never regret that we did too much for them, but we may regret that we could have done more.

> *When people pass out of our life, we will never regret that we did too much for them, but we may regret that we could have done more.*

Life is for living and life is a lesson for the learning.

GOD'S COMMON MIRACLES

I know the plans you have for me
Of blessings poured out from above
Of hope and strength and liberty
My life surrounded by your love

My path at times leads through the dark
And all my dreams quickly remove
I search to gain new strength and find
My life surrounded by your love

My enemies attack from every side
But I will never flee nor move
For I am fixed in faith and hope
My life surrounded by your love

When I approach the golden gate
All heaven's glory now to prove
To bow down at your feet in worship
My life surrounded by your love

Steve Penny May 2003

I cannot read Marion's memories without tears flowing again as it is still so real and graphically embedded as pictures in our minds. These pictures will remain with us as living memories of a challenging journey of faith. It became a journey into a long dark valley of extreme trial and stress and one that we were in some ways not prepared for.

However as we began to walk this challenging road we noticed continually that God was going ahead of us and littering our road with funny little miracles.

Even though we were shocked and surprised by the suddenness of Andrew's sickness, we soon realised that God was not at all taken by surprise but had prepared everything we needed ahead of time so that we could make it through.

Everywhere we looked it seemed as though there were little miracles shining like beacons on our path showing us that God was still with us.

It was obvious that God was not taken by surprise by Andrew's sickness, or by our inept ability to walk daily in faith. He knew exactly what we would need long before we needed them.

Let me share how we recognised some of these natural developments which turned out to be far more than just lucky breaks or coincidences.

One such area of personal excitement for us was our decision at the start of 2003 to knock down our little two bedroom house near the beach and build a nice big house for our family to live in for the future. We had settled

> *It was obvious that God was not taken by surprise by Andrew's sickness, or by our inept ability to walk daily in faith.*

on a builder, had signed a contract to commence building, and had found a rental property to live in for the next eight months. It was within those next few weeks that Andrew's condition was diagnosed and he was rushed to hospital. From that moment nothing made sense any longer. It didn't seem appropriate to continue building a nice big house which would require much time and effort, when our beloved son was now in hospital with a life threatening disease. I couldn't imagine planning and dreaming about our future new home when everything we had looked forward to involving our children, including Andrew and Anna, now seemed to be under threat. So I cancelled the contract on our new house. I also cancelled the rental property that we had secured, and thought to stay in our little house until we knew what the future held.

A few days later, while I was praying and reading my Bible, God directed me to the scriptures in the Book of Nehemiah (Nehemiah 4:14) where it says to fight for your brothers and sisters; your sons and daughters; and to fight for your houses and land. I clearly heard God speak to me from this verse and encourage me to proceed with my dreams – which was the construction of the new house for our family.

To do so, we had to knock the little house down and live in a rental property as originally planned. I went back to the rental agency to see if they had any properties. Amazingly they still had our original rental property available! This was a surprise and a huge blessing, as it was on the outskirts of Caloundra and meant that our access to the highway for travel to and from the Brisbane hospital was much easier. We were to make this tiring journey almost every day for the next seven months.

The house had five bedrooms – two at one end and three at the other end - and was on nearly one acre of land with a full size tennis court and beautiful in-ground pool. The bedroom lay out was absolutely perfect considering what was to develop later – when Andrew would come home from hospital for a few weeks at a time and could use the front two bedrooms with his wife Anna and the rest of our family used the rear three bedrooms. The layout of this house was absolutely perfect for our "season of sickness."

We call this house our "sickness house" as it was the place we lived during Andrew's battle with cancer. However we again thank God that He directed us to continue building our own house near the beach as we were able to leave our sickness house behind and move on to new things.

In December, just a few months after Andrew died, we were able to move out of our "sickness house" with all its sad memories and into our new house prepared for our future. Again I am amazed at how God thinks of everything.

Another miracle of God's design was our sudden choice of a different type of motor vehicle, prior to us learning of Andrew's illness. I had been driving four wheel drive vehicles for a few years and had enjoyed them immensely, but decided for some reason to swap to a larger limousine style car to use for the next 12 months. I had no reason to think this way, but in the months to come it became clear that the Lord had again ordered our steps even in the practical issues of transport.

When Andrew came home from hospital in between his chemo-therapy sessions, he still had to go back into the hospital most days for all kinds of blood transfusions and other procedures, and he was by this time very sick and could hardly walk. Had we still had a four wheel drive vehicle, he would never have been able to get up into them, let alone survive the long trips on such hard seats. The limo was perfect for him, as he often lay down on the back seat during the drive home from the hospital. It also became a perfect car for us as we endured the hour long trip down and back every day to and from the hospital. At the very least, the Lord had provided us with as comfortable a ride as possible.

All these funny little miracles began to fall into place and so we knew that God had not been taken by surprise by Andrew's sickness and He was in complete control. That gave us comfort and added to our faith for a positive outcome.

Another simple miracle that really blessed me concerned my birthday present. My birthday is in April and our church staff decided to buy me a very fancy hand held computer and mobile phone all in one, a personal digital assistant (PDA) as it is commonly referred to. It was the latest model and even had its own little keyboard. This was to prove the most amazing gift, as I would spend hours every day at the hospital typing in every thought and feeling we encountered on our journey with Andrew.

I had no idea that Andrew's sickness would stretch out over seven months or that we would spend countless hours and days at his bedside. The gift of the PDA became invaluable during those long days of waiting for Andrew to wake up. The sense of release was immense as I journaled into that tiny little machine my innermost thoughts, including both my hopes and fears. I found that this little machine became my cork which I could remove allowing me to unload all my pent up feelings.

Whether it is a male thing or not, I'm not sure; but I just couldn't seem to let all my emotions just hang out! To me crying didn't solve anything, nor did sitting around talking about every little detail of the disease. I found release in writing my thoughts into this little PDA I held in my hands.

Marion on the other hand needed people to talk to, and would spend time in the Patients and Guests lounge sharing and encouraging all who visited. Our prayer list became very long, as just about every family asked if we would include them in our prayers. Marion was amazing and would often disappear into other rooms to share for a little while with another patient who needed some tender care.

Both of our children were great company for Andrew when they could visit and always brought a cheerful perspective from the outside world. Andrew loved having them sit all over his bed, and most of all, Andrew so looked forward to the times when Anna could come and visit.

I took to writing about everything I saw in the hospital. Even things like the 'Sharps' boxes on the wall where the used needles are stored, could not escape my poetic attention. I took to writing poems and musings about anything and everything. My poetic ability was fairly basic and predictable, but it was my way of describing the tiresome and frustrating hospital procedures in a creative and sometimes amusing way.

The whole experience of Andrew being so ill was incredibly hard and instead of offloading all my thoughts onto some unsuspecting nurse or visiting friend, I had a great little 'digital listener'.

Looking back now I realise that God had given me a tool to record things for future use. There was one period of a week or so where I became a little negative about the hospital system, and so I recorded a whole lot of less than complimentary poems and other writings, however my little computer crashed not long after that and I lost a whole lot of my writings. When I checked, the only writings I had lost were those I had written

> I realised how much more He wants us to grow and to learn how to control our negative emotions.

during my negative slump. I felt God was showing me that He makes provisions for us to show our emotions honesty, but I realised how much more He wants us to grow and to learn how to control our negative emotions.

The gift my staff had given to me was just another evidence of the amazing way God provides for us in every season of our lives. Because I took to writing poems and stories and recording all the different experiences we shared together, we ended up with a living memory of our journey of faith and of Andrew's amazing courage through it all.

> *I am convinced that we are covered continually by God's grace and that His handiwork is constantly being revealed in our daily lives as we acknowledge Him in all things.*

God's miracles are happening continually in our lives and often these miracles are nondescript and common place, but when looked for with the eye of faith, they weave an amazing tapestry of divine love which becomes like a cloak of grace cast over us in our deepest moments of need. This sense of God's presence with us continued to grow as we continued to stumble over these wonderful "accidents of divine love." I am convinced that we are covered continually by God's grace and that His handiwork is constantly being revealed in our daily lives as we acknowledge Him in all things.

Another miracle involved our parking at the hospital. We were at the hospital every day and parking charges were very expensive. Someone suggested we park in a small car-parking area right outside the door to the oncology section where

Andrew was a patient, an area we had been previously unaware of and one that did not charge any fees for parking. This was an incredible help to us financially as we parked there for almost the entire seven months that Andrew was in hospital. When we were unable to park there anymore due to a change in parking rules, we were always able to find somewhere else. It seemed like every day the Lord prepared a place for us and a car park space would be available. A little thing? Not at all, especially when you have a very sick son who can hardly walk. It became another miracle of grace to us all.

Other miracles of divine grace continued to happen on a daily basis. From the time Andrew was admitted to hospital, he seemed to get one great nurse after another. Many of them were committed Christians like us, who also believed and were praying like we were. It was very comforting to know he was so well looked after and it was so wonderful to talk with many of these highly trained yet soft and sensitive nurses - especially about the things of the Lord. If you can believe it, there were days in the room when it was a joy to be together sharing with some of these wonderful servants of God.

I guess I have become even more convinced of God's amazing grace through everything that has happened. I have learnt to look at everything that happens with an expectation for good, and keep my eyes open for what I call "tokens for good."

These are the everyday evidences of God at work in our lives and they seem to pop up all the time. The only catch is that you have to look for them. They can be easily overlooked and ignored, but if we look for them we will find them everywhere around us.

Everyday events become miracles of God's grace when viewed with the expectation of faith. We learnt to recognise these little miracles early on in our journey of faith, and so we were always being pleasantly surprised by God's "tokens for good" as we walked this challenging journey of faith.

Another amazing miracle of God's unique design happened during the year before Andrew got sick. He had quite a serious accident in his car which shook him up considerably and so he took out a life insurance policy for both sickness and accident cover. This was quite a step as Andrew and Anna were setting up a graphic design business and did not have any spare money at the time.

Consequently, when Andrew died Anna received an insurance payout which has been able to set her up for the next season of her life.

I have come to understand that God is able to see the big picture for our lives and therefore He plans things that seem totally unrelated when they happen, but turn out to be acts of divine pre-planning as the journey unfolds. God's planning for Anna's future is just another evidence of the sovereign ability of God to work all things together for good. I am amazed how God thinks of everything, and what we saw as an accident became a step toward a greater miracle in our lives. Consistently as we were travelling through our dark valley of trials, we found that God had littered the pathway with tokens of His extreme love.

We have learnt never to become so focused on our problem that we stop looking for the evidences of God's continuing presence

> *Everyday events become miracles of God's grace when viewed with the expectation of faith.*

with us. He is always there and His love tokens are continually materialising around us.

It is all about our perspective on life. We made a choice as our journey unfolded to try and look at our circumstance with a faith perspective, and not be blinded by the obvious difficulties and challenges before us. As we looked for evidences of God's grace toward us we were always rewarded with another token for good strategically placed for us to find and enjoy.

When we look back on this incredible season of challenge, we realise that the Bible is so true where it declares;

'The steps of a good man are ordered by the LORD...'
(Psalm37:23& 24)

I am not perfect by any means, or always good, but I chose a journey that would lead me to goodness, to righteousness – that is God. When I chose Him and continue to choose Him, He calls me a 'good man' and continually litters my way with evidences of His love for me. This is how these common miracles happen – me wanting God to show the way, and God showing me and confirming I am on the right track by giving me these tokens for good.

Even when the difficult times came our way we knew that God would sustain us and keep us strong because we were attempting to walk the 'faith journey'.

One thing I never fully realised, was just how much the devil hates those who trust in God and seek to do His will, but we were about to find out.

DOGS RUN IN PACKS

Above the noise of pounding waves,
of seas now raging furiously
Above the heat of madding days,
of sights and sounds so curiously
Imbedded in my brain
I turn to see who dares to speak so soft yet insistent
There is still hope

Above the cry of days now lost,
of regrets and tears as rain
Above the hours of labour's cost,
and sorrows ever present pain
Imbedded in my soul
I turn to see who dares to speak so strong yet insistent
There is still hope

Above the dust of markets toil,
of processions going nowhere
Above the clouds of prophetic hype,
and weariness beyond repair
Imbedded in my body
I turn to see who dares to speak so lovingly yet insistent
There is still hope

Steve Penny June 2003

There are seasons in life when everything that can go wrong, does. You just wake up one morning and it seems as if someone has decided that your life should become a nightmare of negative and destructive events. I believe the enemy of our souls does come to invade our lives seeking whom he may devour. He will find anything he can and throw it at us in an attempt to destroy our faith in God. These things are not just co-incidences or a sequence of natural circumstances, but part of an orchestrated attack of the enemy against us. This is what happened to us during the awful year that Andrew was sick. One after the other, they seemed to come like a pack of dogs, seeking to devour our souls and stifle our faith and confidence in God. It started with Andrew's diagnosis of cancer and then, as if a floodgate had been opened, darkness in many forms seemed to cover our lives like a constant blanket of gloomy fog.

Dogs run in packs. They hunt together to steal, kill and destroy. Our papers in Australia are often telling the story of dogs who have teamed up to attack some poor person inflicting horrible injuries. A normally nice docile animal can change its behaviour when included in a pack of dogs on the prowl.

When Jesus was on the cross of Calvary giving His life for our salvation, He was surrounded by demonic beings described in the Bible by the Psalmist (Psalm 22:16) as being like a pack of dogs. This simply means that trouble comes in packs. The enemy of our souls, the devil, has no power over a righteous person, but he will send his dogs every so often to hound and harass you, to see what you are made of.

It may seem odd that blessing and struggle come together – but they can. Our lives are not often all blessing or all struggle. God works within the struggle – He orders the steps of a good (righteous) man and brings blessing despite the circumstances, but the enemy still attempts to disillusion you and destroy your ability to have any faith, hope or love.

No sooner had we received Andrew's news, than we learnt of at least four other people connected to our church who had also been given a cancer verdict. Some of these good people died during the year, adding to our sorrow and loss. My mother in Adelaide also became ill. She had knocked her hand whilst gardening, which set off severe arthritis in her body. She came to visit and stayed with us during the year, but was quite unwell and looked decidedly frail.

At the same time a small group of people in our church decided to oppose the plans we had for our church future, and began to agitate and spread malicious rumors throughout the church and community. For the rest of the year, these people agitated and maligned the church and its leadership.

They caused us much grief because we loved them, but the pain of their deceit and rejection, compounded with our grief over our eldest son's condition, was almost unbearable. It was beneficial to all that they finally found somewhere else to attend church. During this whole ordeal, my natural instinct was to fight back as I wanted to defend not only myself, but the church. What was happening seemed so unjust and completely inconceivable. But the Lord told me not to fight back nor defend our position, as it was His fight. In the book of Nehemiah, God says that He will fight against those who oppose the builders of His house – that is the church (Nehemiah 2:20). So we remained silent as these unfair and unfounded criticisms continued to gather momentum around us.

For the first time since assuming the leadership of our church, there was division in the camp, and I was powerless to do anything about it except give it over to the Lord - God had to work it out.

Suddenly in May, Marion's mum Heather died of a heart attack. It came as a complete shock to us all. She had been in good health and was a great friend and support to Marion - as was Marion to her. We were devastated when we received the phone call from Marion's brother Tom. In the middle of what was already a dark gloomy night this phone call just shattered us. That night is one we definitely won't forget.

Heather's funeral was a positive and joyous occasion for all who knew her. She had been such a faithful servant of the Lord over her whole life, serving with her husband George as church leaders, and so there were many family and friends gathered to celebrate her life of faith. However for Marion, Heather's funeral was just another huge blow, and incredibly difficult; as she and her mum were very close. Heather had been Marion's confidante and friend and now she was gone in our deepest hour of need.

To me it just didn't seem right. I really struggled with God's timing over Heather's death. It just could not have happened to us at a worse time in our lives. Marion needed her mother as a sounding board and an encourager when the going was rough. It should not have happened this way and I had to deal with my attitude toward God over what I considered was divine ineptness. Marion did not even have time to mourn her mother's passing, as Andrew was home from hospital for a few days and so she needed to get back quickly for him and continue being strong.

Then another blow was delivered. The group of unhappy people in our church, who had caused us much grief already with their lies, became so hostile that they went to the newspapers to have their deceit published. Whilst we were having some refreshments following Heather's funeral, we received a phone call from the local newspaper advising us that they would be running a front page feature article on our church containing the lies spread by our group of dissidents.

> I had to
> deal with
> my attitude
> toward God
> over what I
> considered
> was divine
> ineptness.

What a time to receive such a phone call! Thankfully, we have a very good reputation in our community and our solicitors were able to persuade the newspaper that it would not be in their best interests to spread such obvious untruths, and so they decided not to publish their front page story.

I felt as though darkness was enveloping my soul from every side. I wondered when all these attacks would end. It was then that I heard a strange voice inside saying that another one of our children (other than Andrew) would also die.

It chilled me to the core and I began to have fear attacks whenever one of our children was even a few minutes late. I knew this was just another attack of the enemy and that I must not let him dominate my life. I had to get these mind games under control.

God helped me to overcome these panic attacks as I spent time with Him in the early hours each morning finding promises in my Bible and praying to God. As I sat and rested and tried to relax in God's presence I found that His promises of a good outcome became real to me. When I was in God's presence I knew everything would be okay. However, it was a hard road to walk out. There were many attacks during that awful period and it became very challenging to keep believing that all things would work together for good. Morbid thoughts would attack my mind at the most unexpected moments and I found it most disconcerting and very difficult some days to carry on with my normal duties.

Why am I telling you all this? Because the devil and his dogs love to hunt in packs and they often come as a relentless flood of faith-stealing, hope-robbing, love-bashing attacks and he won't stop with just one outburst.

We also experienced a number of people calling on us during the time of Andrew's sickness all selling their amazing health products. To me it was uncanny how they heard about our predicament and all arrived with amazing stories of wonder products able to cure anything. They came from everywhere. We decided to buy some of the products and see if Andrew could keep any of the stuff down. This was impossible as he was unable to keep any form of food down for more than a few minutes.

One day we persuaded him to take one of the wonder potions only to find him in tears early in the morning having had an attack of diahhorea; but being barely able to walk, he had suffered an accident in his attempt to reach the ensuite toilet. We vowed never to force him to do such a thing again.

We also allowed another local distributor of health products to come and talk to us regarding the potential of their product to assist the body in fighting cancer. We dragged Andrew out of bed to listen to his story, and then realised we had become prisoners to an insensitive salesman who went on and on and on with his wonder presentation. Rudeness was the only way we could evict this peddler of potions from our home. We said sorry again to Andrew and struggled to carry him back to bed.

I must say here, that some of these distributors were decent caring people who honestly wanted to help, and some of their products helped Marion and I, as we battled exhaustion and fatigue. To these people we say thank you for your love and genuine support. However it was just so incredible that some took advantage of our son's illness and our desperation to try anything that we were assured would help. I am amazed that some people could have an ulterior motive even when dealing with people struggling to find answers in their hour of deepest need.

Let me simply say that dogs sometimes come in the form of people who seem to have a personal reason to viciously attack or exploit you; sometimes in the form of circumstances where things just go wrong, and then sometimes in straight out unseen spiritual attacks, especially attacks on your mind through oppressive thoughts; but if you stand firm and resolute and just keep on believing that God will work it out, you will find that none of these things can separate you from the love of God.

The Apostle Paul said, "beware of dogs," and he had good reason to say it. We must be on our guard continually for those things that will rob us of our joy and peace in life.

Let me share some things I learned about how to handle these unwanted dog attacks.

1. NEVER STOOP TO THEIR LEVEL.

Always stand upright and be confident in God. Dogs want to pull you down to their level so they can savage you. Don't go to ground or stoop to their level of life. If you play their game – you will probably lose. Stay standing in the grace of God and soon they will sense you cannot be intimidated or brought down to their earthy level.

2. NEVER GIVE BARKING DOGS UNDUE ATTENTION.

I found that I needed to keep my focus on God and His promises for my life and not let these barking dogs get all my attention. Your negative circumstances will hound you for your attention, and you can soon be expending all your energies keeping them at bay. Do not give them undue attention, and like most dogs, if you stand your ground they will slink away, defeated and exposed for what they really are.

3. STAND YOUR GROUND.

Do not give in to barking dogs. They get a sniff of a truth and turn it into a melee of barking rumors. One barking dog sets off a whole chorus who do not even know why they are barking. When they come barking up a storm just stand your ground and do not give an inch. Stay focused on who you are and what you are called to do in life.

We must be on our guard continually for those things that will rob us of our joy and peace in life.

One of the scriptures in the Bible that became a great encouragement to me is in Romans chapter five and verse two, which says that we can access God's grace through faith.

God's grace is available for me in every situation of life, and I can access it at any time by faith in God and His word. Even when circumstances gang up on me like a pack of dogs, I can stand confident and assured of God's help.

I realised that I needed to step into God's grace and provision by faith, and once there - in a position of believing for God's grace to be sufficient - I must then stand firm and not turn back. I must never give in to my circumstances no matter how powerful or overwhelming. I must do all I can in faith, and having done the best I can with what I have, then I must simply stand firm in the grace of God.

So many other things went wrong during this awful year of challenge, however these are just a few examples to help explain the tactics of the enemy and how I have learnt to not give undue attention to mangy yapping dogs. They are not worth giving our time and energies to.

It was during this awful year that I again realised with an absolute assurance that the steps of a good man are ordered of the Lord. Nothing is beyond His control. Nothing is an accident. In fact everything in God's plan for our lives is redemptive. All things do work together for good.

Life is more than a series of "unrelated incidents" – whether good or bad. When we see life as a series of unrelated incidents we are simply allowing "fate" to have its way, but because I believe in a loving creator God I can never live this way. I am convinced that everything happens for a purpose and everything can be given to God and turned around to become redemptive and positive in our lives.

When we accept that our lives represent a journey of cohesive "shaping events" we can accept the bad times as being a part of a much bigger plan that will ultimately turn out for good. This does not mean that God directs us into bad things but he does lead us through them, and bring us out of them stronger in faith and Christian character.

> *In fact everything in God's plan for our lives is redemptive. All things do work together for good.*

I am often moved by some of the people who attend our church who have been through shocking abuse and associated mental trauma and yet when they share their stories of God's amazing help in their lives they always conclude by declaring that God is helping them to turn all their hurts and distresses into positive qualities for the future.

There is always a highway of hope when we entrust our life to a loving God who cares about us in every way. Because of our belief that God is in control of our lives we chose not to blame God for our awful journey but to turn to Him in simple faith and expect Him to direct our steps out of the dark valley of evil we had been dragged into. No-one is exempt from bad things in this sin cursed world, and often we find ourselves facing things that really are not fair. Accept the fact that life is not always fair – but God is always just. God will always work out His plan of salvation for us if we will call upon Him.

We knew that we could not hold on to resentment and anger against God as though He had personally caused our pain as this would cut us off from the very source of love and help that we needed.

Heaven always has a plan for our lives. Hopelessness is simply not knowing or believing God's plan for our future. No matter how dark and evil your journey is right now, there is hope. Never let go of hope. Never end the journey before your time. Do not ever contemplate suicide. Never stop believing for God's help. Heaven has a plan for us and it is a good plan. God declares that He has a plan for us, and it is for good and not for evil, to give us a future and a hope. (Jeremiah 29:11) Hang on to hope and keep believing that heaven has a plan for our lives and that we can find it.

A GLIMPSE OF HEAVEN

When the way ahead looks dark and foreboding
And every step seems covered by shadows
When the light you once knew seems so far removed
And your testimony's shaken and your faith's being proved
Its time to dig a well

When your days become repetitive and dreary
And your mind is filled with questions
How long will this valley continue to go on?
Until the well gets deeper and the sweeter your song
Keep on digging your well

As my well gets deeper and my faith gets stronger
I see the wisdom of God in all that I do
And I pray for those who will follow behind me
May they drink from this well and find strength to go on
I've finally dug my well

Steve Penny   July 2003

Andrew's condition was deteriorating quickly and we realised that we needed a divine miracle from God, or he would die within days. We had believed God in faith over the past six months, and had done everything we could possibly try. We had studied the internet for many hours searching for every remedy we could find and had tried many different health products, etc. however for us the only real way of faith was to keep praying together and believing God for a miracle.

It was now late August and Andrew had been sent home from the hospital with the sentence over him that he only had weeks to live. His condition was awful and we knew that there was not much time left. At that time a lady in our church gave us a note saying that she believed God had spoken to her, that if we would fast and pray for three days we would see a resurrection on the third day. Our church had been wonderful and had prayed with us for a miracle to happen, and so we decided to ask the church to specifically fast and pray for three days and then come together to pray on the Wednesday night and believe for a great miracle.

The church prayer meeting was to address a number of challenges in our church with Andrew's sickness being just one of a number of serious illnesses represented. Marion and I stayed home with Andrew that night and had a phone connection with the church. Andrew by now was slipping in and out of consciousness. It was a powerful night of prayer as we all prayed fervently together for God's miracle to happen.

We really did feel a surge of faith during our phone hook up with the church and sensed that God was doing something in Andrew's body. After the prayer service Marion's brother Tom came to visit bringing a piece of cloth that the church people had prayed over together. The Bible says this cloth should then be laid on the sick person believing for a miracle. We laid it on Andrew's head and prayed for his complete healing. When we finished praying, Andrew said, "amen" and that was the last intelligible word we heard him say. As we walked out of his room after praying for him we heard him make an unusual groaning sound and we realised he was unconscious. It was ten o'clock at night and he stayed that way until he passed on into heaven the next morning.

I never believed I would ever be able to release Andrew, and I was committed to fight on to the very end; but as we laid the prayer cloth on his head it seemed as though God's peace flooded the room and we found ourselves praying for the Lord to take him home. We all felt it together. It was an unusual strength that we encountered and it enabled us to let Andrew go. I can't explain it any other way than feeling like God was in control and that we could entrust our son into His loving care.

To be honest I actually had to firstly deal with my pride at this point, not wanting to admit defeat in seeing our son die. We had fought so hard for so long and at first it seemed as though we were giving in to the obvious decline in Andrew's condition. However there was no doubt that God was present so we just prayed for God to resurrect Andrew to heaven for all eternity.

As we sat in the lounge for a few minutes with Tom, we realised that Andrew's breathing had changed as he slipped into a deep unconscious state. He spent the night that way. The next morning on Thursday 4th September 2003, at around ten past eight in the morning, our son Andrew died - passing peacefully from this world into the joy of his salvation forever. Our family was present to see him breathe his last breath and pass on into the arms of Jesus Christ. While Andrew was in his last minutes of life and completely unconscious, we just continued to talk to him about spending eternity with Jesus. We all told him how much we loved him and would miss him, and that he was going on ahead to get everything ready for us in heaven.

> *We just prayed for God to resurrect Andrew to heaven for all eternity.*

While this was happening Marion answered a phone call from our palliative care nurse who had rung to see how Andrew was going. Marion said, "I think he is dying right now." The nurse asked if we wanted her to come and we all agreed she should come as soon as possible. She came and was able to help us deal with Andrew's final few minutes of life. Once Andrew had breathed his last she felt Andrew's neck and established that there was no pulse and declared that Andrew had passed on. She then left us to share our sorrow together.

She bumped into Marion just a week or so after Andrew died and said, "You all handled Andrew's death so well." We didn't feel as though we had done anything special except that we were all calm and peaceful, encouraging one another in Andrew's promotion to heaven. We just handled our moment of sorrow as best we could and comforted one another with our Christian hope.

However, it is still the most gut-wrenching thing I have ever experienced. No one should have to see their children die in their arms and leave this earth ahead of them. The sense of sorrow and loss is beyond description. You feel like you have lost a part of yourself and indeed you have, and it can never be replaced. As Andrew lay there now motionless, a cavalcade of memories began their procession through my mind. One after the other they passed before me stirring up deep emotions as these precious memories seemed to all be saying farewell until another time.

When Luke came into the room just after Andrew had breathed his last we just hugged and sobbed uncontrollably for a little while, and then reassured each other that Andrew was now in heaven with Jesus.

Anna, Andrew's wife was so gentle and loving as she stroked Andrew's face and said her farewells. I was so moved for Anna at this point and asked the Lord to help her in a special way in her hour of grief. And yet for all of us, our sorrow was tempered just a little by our Christian hope. We had lived all our lives with the hope of heaven held before us, and here we were realising it was now much more than words. There was a sense of peace and calm in the room as we prayed and released our son, assuring him that we would see him again soon in a better place. We knew that Andrew had committed his life to Christ and had an assurance of his faith.

The fact that Andrew had intelligently and specifically asked God to forgive him of his sins through believing in Jesus Christ as his saviour; meant more to us as parents than if he had won gold at an Olympic Games. Andrew was forgiven by God and had received Jesus Christ into his life. I knew he would be in heaven waiting for me when I arrived. This hope helped carry me through my time of grief over his physical parting.

Even though our tears flowed unceasingly from that time on, we knew that our tears were just a part of our healing that needed to take place this side of heaven. God actually showed me that tears can be like a river flowing through the human soul washing away grief, bitterness and hurt. To stifle this flow is to hinder God's healing process in the human soul. Our tears weren't really about Andrew being in heaven but more about us missing him here on earth. I love the fact that the Bible says there will be no more tears in heaven, because He shall wipe away all tears from our eyes. (Revelation 7:17)

I don't know how people can face the finality of eternity without the assurance that they are right with God. I cannot comprehend how people face life, let alone death, without knowing the one who came to give us life and who conquered over the power of the grave. I am so glad that Jesus has broken the finality and sorrow of death, and we were now experiencing the "blessed hope" of heaven firsthand.

Being touched by death in such an untimely way, has changed the way I look at life. No one can boast of tomorrow, and eternity becomes so much more real when someone you love has crossed over. The most wonderful thing about the Christian faith is the fact that death no longer has any finality about it. It is simply a transition to a new dimension to spend the rest of eternity in the presence of God and His angels. We knew that Andrew was ready to meet his Saviour, and the truth is, our sorrow was more about us and our loss, rather than for Andrew who we knew had received great gain.

> *We prayed and released our son, assuring him that we would see him again soon in a better place.*

Just the week before Andrew went to heaven, I talked to him about eternity. He said he was scared to die naturally, and wondered how death happened; and yet he knew if he did die he was going to heaven. He actually was more worried about Anna being left alone, and made us promise to do whatever we could to help her get on with her life. We talked about heaven and what it would be like, and especially the fact that God had taken Ma (Marion's mum, Heather) home first to be there waiting for him. Andrew was very fond of Ma. Poppa – my dad – was also in heaven and we joked about meeting Poppa as well. God thinks of everything.

> *Our tears were just a part of our healing that needed to take place this side of heaven.*

I have preached this blessed hope of heaven all over the world for many years but now it has become so much more real to all of us. We have entered into the joy of our salvation and know that our son Andrew is waiting for us in heaven to spend eternity together.

And yet the loss is immense. There is still not a day goes by that I do not have moments when I think Andrew should be included in my activities, and fresh tears overflow like a river reminding me again of our earthly loss. I find it so hard to play golf now as Andrew was my golfing partner. I still start crying for no reason whenever I play golf as I look up expecting to see Andrew enjoying the game with me. He and I loved to watch sport together on TV and now there is an empty chair in the room. The loss of a dear companion and friend is like a dull ache embedded in the soul.

However God was so gracious to me in a most unusual way in giving me a glimpse of eternity to assure me of our son's blessed state: I was in the city of Bergen in Norway, in February 2004, just five months after Andrew had died, and was there to speak at a church conference. During the worship session in one of the services, I had a vision which was totally unexpected and quite amazing. It was just like God opened my eyes and I saw a vision of my son Andrew riding on the back of two angels. He was straddling the two angels and holding onto their wings as he left earth's atmosphere and disappeared into the clouds above. It was remarkable because he looked so frail and sickly as he started his ascent, and then he became progressively stronger and more majestic as he rode on angel's wings up into the heavens. As he disappeared from view he looked just so glorious. By the time he had reached the clouds he was riding on the backs of the angels like an ancient gladiator in a chariot. I just burst into tears and then felt embarrassed as I looked around and found myself back in the worship service realising my emotion didn't fit the order of the service. I had not been thinking about Andrew and so the vision came as a complete shock to me.

No sooner had I stopped crying than God opened my eyes again and I saw another vision. This was a scene of people sitting around the throne of Christ in heaven. I didn't actually see the Lord on His throne, but just knew it was Him. Seated around Him were many people singing with all their might.

The most wonderful thing about the Christian faith is the fact that death no longer has any finality about it.

However my attention was drawn to a person in the front row. I knew it was Andrew yet it did not look like him naturally. I just knew it was him, and wonder of wonders, he was singing his lungs out in worship to the Lord. Just as I began to comprehend the scene, Andrew turned around to look at me, (as I was standing behind the group.) He turned and saw me and gave me the biggest grin as only he could. It was a smile of a child who has been given their greatest desire and I knew immediately it was our son. He then turned back toward the throne of Christ and continued singing with complete enthusiasm and joy. Then the scene vanished and I was again back in the worship service in Bergin, Norway.

God had for some reason allowed me to see my son in heaven and it has had a remarkable impact on my life. I can never be the same. I have now seen my first son enjoying heaven, and every prayer we have prayed, and every moment spent sharing about the Lord, has been more than worth it. To have seen just a glimpse of heaven, has more than satisfied my soul that it will be worth it all when we finally get to heaven and see our Saviour face to face. I can rest confidently that the first member of our immediate family is already in heaven enjoying catching up with his grandparents and other loved ones. I can't wait to get to heaven. It will be just so absolutely glorious. My passion now is to help as many people as possible live life on earth with the blessed assurance that heaven is their destination when they pass into eternity forever. I have realised now, that even though I may have initially become a Christian as a young boy to escape hell and its eternal torment, I now live today as a Christian because I want to spend eternity with Jesus Christ. My understanding of the Christian life is so much different since I have witnessed and felt a little bit of heaven. Nothing can ever satisfy you on the inside like a moment in the presence of Christ.

Whatever experiences we may have here on earth, I can assure you, there is nothing to compare with the amazing sense of completeness and fulfilment you feel in the presence of Christ. If I could put into words the highest sense of accomplishment I have ever felt on earth, it would pale into insignificance compared to the brief moment I experienced in my vision of heaven.

I now understand a little more of what the great Apostle Paul, who wrote most of the Bible's New Testament epistles, meant when he said, *"for me to live is Christ and to die is gain."* *(Philippians 1:21)* If I am to live a little longer here on earth then it will be to serve my Lord and Saviour Jesus Christ; and were I to be taken from this world into the next; then for me it would be considered as a positive gain.

I have at times wanted to go to heaven since I have seen these visions, but I know that my work on earth is not yet finished and that we have two other wonderful children whom the Lord has given to us. We want to help them fulfill their godly destiny and make a difference this side of eternity. It is too late once you cross over.

We only have one life to live as there are no dress rehearsals in life. I have realised afresh that life is actually about preparing for eternity and so I am even more committed to serving God here on earth before I go to heaven. I want to leave the fingerprint of God on as many lives as possible before I go to heaven to enjoy extreme bliss and fulfilment forever and ever.

It is amazing to me how often our lives are touched by heaven in some tangible way. When I was 12 years of age my mother died due to a massive hemorrhage from a tubule pregnancy. She was pronounced dead, but was miraculously brought back to life by a minister praying over her dead body. During those moments when my mother was suspended between heaven and earth she sensed God's presence in a profound way and a deep peace flooded her being. I can remember times when my mother would share a little of these experiences and it always raised the hairs on the back of my head.

> *Nothing can ever satisfy you on the inside like a moment in the presence of Christ.*

Another time when heaven seemed so close was during Marion's cancer scare not long after we were married.

> *Heaven is designed to reflect and show off the amazing beauty and majesty of Jesus Christ.*

She was diagnosed with breast cancer and was immediately rushed into hospital for surgery. This was my first real challenge concerning death and eternity and I remember feeling so ill prepared for the after life. I was terribly fearful of losing Marion and did not have a real peace about the beauty and majesty of heaven as her destination. Thankfully God healed her and has allowed Marion to continue the journey with me here on planet earth.

Now I feel totally different about heaven and the after life. Death has lost its sting and the grave has no power over me. I know there is a place called heaven which is so full of the presence of God that it is indescribable with human words.

Heaven centres on Jesus Christ. He fills heaven with His presence. Heaven is designed to reflect and show off the amazing beauty and majesty of Jesus Christ. Without Jesus heaven would be incomplete.

When I saw the amazing look on our son Andrew's face as he worshipped Jesus, I understood how heaven is filled with everything good from God. Complete fulfilment and joy are the words I would use to describe how it will feel to be in heaven. I want everyone who reads this book to make sure you are ready for heaven. Get your life right with God through Jesus Christ, God's only son. He is the Saviour of the world, and he is the light and life of heaven. To know Jesus is to know life eternal and to enjoy it forever in his presence.

If you do not have an assurance of heaven when you die, then invite Jesus Christ into your life right now and begin living a life of hope and purpose which will last for eternity.

If you would like to invite Jesus Christ into your life as your Saviour for all eternity then pray this prayer from your heart.

Dear Heavenly Father,
I know that you love me, because you sent your Son Jesus Christ to die for my sins.
I confess I have sinned and come short of your standards.
I ask you Lord Jesus to come into my life; forgive me and cleanse me from all sin.
Please fill me with your Holy Spirit and empower me to live a Godly life.
I receive you now as my Lord and Saviour and will live for you from this moment on.
I look forward to spending eternity in your presence.
Amen

FAITH, HOPE & LOVE

When the trials of life surround you
and your eyes no longer see
And the hope you once held strongly
seems a distant memory
Its time to lift up your head and shout out His name
I'm not just a number and life's not just a game
All my days have been counted by my Father above
So I'll focus again on faith, hope and love.

When the pain you feel increases
and there's no relief in sight
When your path seems filled with sadness
and your days like darkest night
It's time to lift up your head and shout out His name
I'm not just a number and life's not just a game
All my days have been counted by my Father above
So I'll focus again on faith, hope and love.

When your dreams no longer stir you
and no hope they ever bring
When your soul no longer lifts itself
to fly on eagle's wings
It's time to lift up your head and shout out His name
I'm not just a number and life's not just a game
All my days have been counted by my Father above
So I'll focus again on faith, hope and love.

Andrew's condition swung up and down like a roller coaster ride. After some treatments of chemo his cancer counts would come right down and we would all rejoice. Our faith was working and God was in control. Then without warning the counts would jump up again and we would all be thrown into confusion and dismay. We would start asking, why isn't the miracle happening the way we expected? And so our journey of faith continued. Day after day! Week after week! Month after month! Until we started to feel tired and wrung out from the fight. It was then that we realised that we must learn to trust God and let Him do the fighting for us, and we began to learn in a far clearer way how our faith must work in the midst of our trials.

As this valley of the shadow of death began to cast its dark shadow over us we realised we had to keep our faith in God alive when everything around us seemed to be dying. Everything we had taught others about faith now became our tutor. It was like going from the classroom into an apprenticeship where you actually have to do the things you have learnt. I thank God for the great lessons of faith we had learnt over many years, and now we knew we would have to instinctively live these faith principles in a battle of life and death. Our faith actually grew as we stood firm - believing God and His promises for our lives. We knew that God was well able to do what we were asking and we expected it to happen every day. We did everything we had been taught to do to see a miracle happen in Andrew's life.

We confessed God's word daily. I found Bible verses that promised healing and health and declared them out loud throughout the day. We also prayed continually. We had many of our friends who are great men of faith come and pray personally for Andrew. We stood firm in our faith and consistently practiced giving glory to God. I would take time to praise God and declare His great attributes and continually be thankful for all He had done for us. We expected a miracle. I believed God had given me a promise that Andrew would serve with me in the ministry. I held on to this promise with everything I had. Yet still Andrew's condition deteriorated, despite three courses of the strongest chemo possible.

And then the unthinkable; Andrew died on the 4th September 2003 and our whole world was again turned upside down. I declared to our church and to our friends that faith always triumphs and God is always in control, and I truly believed what I said, but somehow the words Andrew spoke to Marion rang in our ears continually. He had been at home for a few days and was having a very bad time of it, when the doctors finally gave us the news that the latest course of chemo had failed and the cancer was returning very aggressively. Andrew just broke down and cried as Marion tried to encourage him. He then blurted out. "Where's the miracle, aren't we believing for a miracle?"

Those words continued to haunt me after Andrew's passing. I believed that God could and would heal him; we spoke it out, we prayed it out, we thought it out – and yet healing didn't happen. Did we not have faith? Did Andrew think we didn't have faith? I just didn't understand what God was doing. I just didn't feel like I understood faith anymore. Faith believes and trusts in God for things we do not see or understand, and we were certainly doing that!

One day I asked the Lord to teach me how faith can still work when we don't see the miracle the way we wanted to see it. I had always had a fairly simple understanding of faith. To me faith consisted of getting a promise from God and believing it with everything I had until it came to pass. My expression of faith was more about personal boldness and tenacity than a genuine trust in God's unfailing love for me.

Over a period of time the Lord began to show me how faith, together with hope and love, can all work together to achieve a good outcome for those who love God. Faith is not just a "Christian" formula but is a gift from God to every human being, and begins in our lives with the desire and ability to reach out in search of our creator God. Every person on the planet can exercise this level of faith because the Bible declares that God has put eternity within the hearts of every human being born on planet earth. This is why most people at some time in their life search for spiritual meaning and purpose.

Many people have found a genuine relationship with God through searching for Him in their deep hour of need. The Bible says that God has never forsaken any of us, but is always there waiting for us to call out to Him in our distress. Once we find God and enter into a relationship with Him, our faith begins to grow and we can then believe for things once thought impossible and beyond our reach.

Over the course of my committed Christian life I have experienced my faith growing as I have learnt to look for God's help in all kinds of situations. Faith is not only there when we need help in bad times, but is also within us so we can progress in life and possess all kinds of blessings and accomplishments. It is also possible for us to "fail in faith" when trying to accomplish something beyond our natural ability. Every one of us has at times "failed in faith" whilst attempting something impossible.

The Bible says that faith cannot fail because it is a gift from God, but we can "fail in our attempts to walk in faith." In fact there are occasions almost daily when the perfect plans of faith in our life do not come to pass. When we get sick, or miss an opportunity, or have an argument with someone, we are failing in our walk of faith. It is in these times that we realise we are still growing in faith and confidence, and we

> *Faith, together with hope and love, can all work together to achieve a good outcome for those who love God.*

need to get up and get on with life. I find it easy to get up again when it is only a small "failure in faith", but it becomes a lot harder when it is something of greater impact and loss in our lives. Unfortunately some people give up on God and their faith in these times and walk away from God in discouragement.

After Andrew died I was "comforted" by a number of people saying how much they felt for us seeing that our "faith had not worked." This really upset me as I realised it would be impossible for me to continue to believe in God and trust Him, if the faith He had given me did not work. Something was not right and I needed to find out from the Bible how I could continue trusting and believing in God when things had apparently failed.

Over the next few pages I want to teach you my "theology of failure" and explain what to do when things don't work out as planned. These thoughts have been so liberating and have really helped us to rest in God during the months following Andrew's death, and now as time goes on, they are helping us to begin standing up again into new levels of faith and favour. Most people don't want to talk about these painful "failures in faith", and often shut them out and try to soldier on, but I want to show you from the Bible how you can continue to live and overcome after these so called "failures". This revelation has set us free to go on in faith and see even greater victories happen in our lives, even after what appeared to be our worst failure of faith.

> *The Bible says that faith cannot fail because it is a gift from God, but we can "fail in our attempts to walk in faith."*

Amazingly we have seen more miracles of God's favour and blessing in the months following Andrew's death than perhaps ever before. I will show you how to rise up in fresh faith even while other people are still feeling sorry for you, and maybe even condemning you. You can go forward and upward in life even after the worst apparent disaster, failure and loss.

My 'theology of failure' came about as I was studying the following verse in the Bible, after hearing the Lord speak to me that the greatest thing in the world is His love. I started looking into scriptures regarding God's love and stumbled across this little verse, which came alive to me in a whole new way.

1 Corinthians 13:13, "And now abide faith, hope, love, these three: but the greatest of these is love."

All of a sudden it dawned on me that these three essentials were connected together as one. Like the trinity, three yet one. God is a three part being (called the 'Trinity') yet still one in being and function. God the Father, God the Son, and God the Holy Spirit; three yet one!

I saw it. Just as God is three yet one, so faith to be complete is three, yet one. The Trinity of faith has three distinct facets – faith, hope and love. These three must work together in our lives to see the plan of God completed in us. The Trinity is three in one and so is faith, and each member of the trinity has a unique role to play in our expression of faith.

> *I will show you how to rise up in fresh faith even while other people are still feeling sorry for you, and maybe even condemning you.*

God never does anything without each member of the Trinity contributing equally. When God created the heavens and the earth the Bible declares that each member of the Trinity had a unique role to play. So it is when it comes to us living by faith. God the Father, God the Son and God the Holy Spirit each contribute and play their part in helping us to live a wonderful life of faith.

The Bible says that, "without faith it is impossible to please God," and so each member of the Trinity works to help us live a life of faith. This three part expression of the Trinity working together is seen in many different ways throughout the Bible, just as faith's three parts also work in unity together in our lives for good. It blew me away as it dawned on me how these three parts of faith actually work.

LOVE is the foundation   LOVE TRUSTS
HOPE is the building   HOPE BELIEVES
FAITH is the expression   FAITH ACTS

I couldn't believe it. It seemed so obvious and I was amazed that I had never seen how these three facets of faith work together and grow progressively in our lives. We are to progress from a position of being seated in the Father's love, to standing up into the fullness of Christ, and then progressing to a life of walking in the power of the Holy Spirit.

LOVE TRUSTS   SIT - in the Father's love
HOPE BELIEVES   STAND - in Christ's fullness

But it must first begin with love. Our Christian life begins as we learn to sit in the Father's love. I had to learn to trust God and know that He is God and that He is able to do anything at all in my life. Love must be the foundation of everything we do in life. Our love for God must underpin every facet of our Christian walk. The enemy of our souls will always try to destroy our foundation of love for God.

Psalm 11:3 declares, "If the foundations are destroyed, what can the righteous do?"

Our foundation is a love that trusts. The moment we stop trusting is the moment our love starts dying. God eternally loves us and we can always love Him.

I was starting to get excited as I looked into the Bible for more proof of God's plan for me, and I found some amazing scriptures which talked about love that trusts.

Psalm 13:5: "But I trust in your unfailing love: my heart rejoices in your salvation."

To trust in God's unfailing love is the beginning and end of every successful Christian life. The unfailing love of our heavenly Father is the foundation of all our faith and works. We really had to come back to this when Andrew got sick. Did God still love us? Was there an issue in our lives that God was dealing with? Could we continue to pray with confidence that God would perform a miracle? At the end of the day we just had to decide to trust God because of His great love for us. End of story! God either loves us unconditionally or He doesn't. We decided to trust.

Psalm 20:7: "Some trust in chariots and some in horses, but we trust in the name of the Lord our God."

Psalm 52:8: "But I am like an olive tree flourishing in the House of God; I trust in God's unfailing love for ever and ever."

The Bible is full of scriptures that support the truth that LOVE TRUSTS. Love is the foundation of all faith and we were learning again that we need strong foundations, especially when you watch someone you love slowly dying before your eyes challenging everything you have ever believed about faith. There were times when we would just look at each other and say, "It is up to God, all we can do is trust Him."

When a baby is born to loving earthly parents it immediately looks toward the parents with a love that trusts implicitly. Where did this loving trust come from? It is given from God as part of His gift of faith. Watch the little child as it begins to develop and grow. Even in an imperfect family environment the little child will return to flawed parents over and over again with a love that trusts and believes for good. How much more love will we find when we look for the love of our perfect Heavenly Father.

We are all created to love and trust our Heavenly Father because it is part of our DNA. God created us to love and trust Him and even though we now live in a sinful and broken world we are still made in His image and we still want to return to Him and trust in His unfailing love forever. Now come to the scripture that really nailed this trust thing for me.

Proverbs 3:5: "Trust in the Lord with all your heart and lean not to your own understanding."

Wow! God was commanding me to trust in the Lord with all my heart – not my head. Why? Because my heart is for loving – not my head! It is only my heart that has the capacity to trust God - not my head. In fact we are commanded not to lean on our own understanding as we will always struggle with trust if we keep relying on our reason.

When we visited the hospital every day and spent all our time staring at sickness and death, our mind became our greatest enemy. We looked at the facts and watched Andrew dying, and focused on the reports of cancer counts increasing. It screamed its logic at us as loud as it could and demanded that the verdicts we make be rational and realistic.

This battle to trust God was one of the most difficult fights to win, as it was an ongoing daily bombardment. In the end I just had to choose to trust God no matter what each day presented. Our heart is the eternal part of our makeup and it is the only part of us that can understand the eternal. It is the spirit part of us that connects us to God and to His eternal world. The Bible says we can only understand the eternal realm by faith. This is very important as we cannot comprehend eternal and spiritual things with our natural mind. It does not compute! No savvy! Cannot understand!

Spiritual things require faith to be understood. This is the reason some people struggle to believe and trust in God. They feel that they must work it out in their mind and consequently struggle because our mind just is not capable of comprehending eternity.

> *To trust in God's unfailing love is the beginning and end of every successful Christian life.*

We must understand and accept eternity and God by faith. A miracle cannot be understood with our human mind because it is beyond natural reason. We can acknowledge that it has happened but we are incapable of understanding and explaining it.

To overcome every situation in life requires us to make a choice to love and trust God with all our heart, and

Luke, Sheree, Andrew

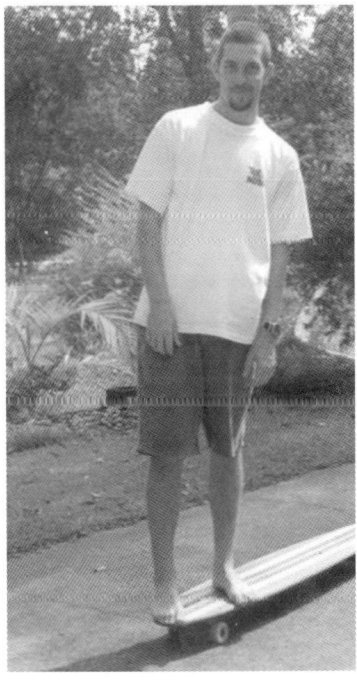

Andrew at age 11   "Toes on the nose" skateboarding

Andrew and Anna at home

Guitar lessons

Andrew at age 25

The happy bride and groom

The family at the wedding

Marion and Sheree with 'Ma'

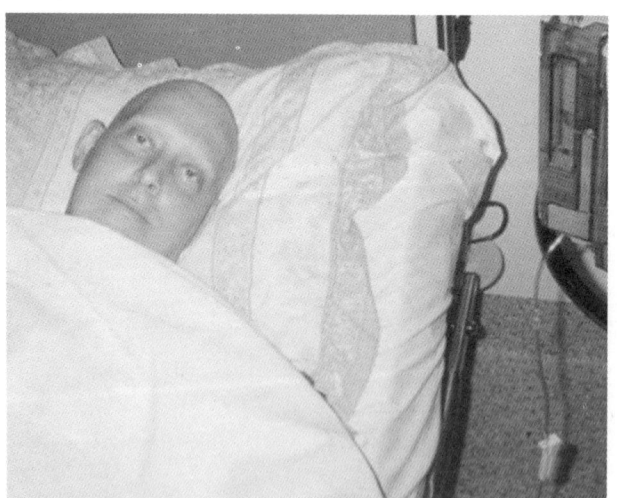

Andrew in hospital

to ignore the demand for reason from our natural mind. In my mind I could not accept that a loving God needed to take my son home to heaven at twenty-seven years of age. Why? What reason could he possibly have? My mind staggered and refused to help me believe in faith. My mind resisted any of my attempts to have faith. Then I realised that my mind is not the breeding ground for faith. God has put eternity in my heart and it is from my heart that I choose to love and trust God. After that I can start to get my thinking sorted out.

Even in our natural life it is true that we do not love someone with our mind but with our heart. Imagine explaining to someone that you are in love with them because of six very practical reasons. No! This is not love. Love is the intangible that sweeps us off our feet and makes us act a little crazy and even trust when logic says take care. Trust is the infallible proof of love. You can't say you love someone if you don't trust them. What we love we trust implicitly.

When we love God and learn to sit in His love, it is shown by our trust in Him. The beginning of our Christian faith is found in our simple love for God. We want to enjoy His presence and get to know Him better. When I spent time every morning reading the Bible and praying, it was like I was climbing up onto God's knee and spending time with Him.

Consider how often a little child wants to be picked up and held by loving parents. There is a bonding that has taken place and the little child feels very safe and secure in the arms of a loving parent. It is not a rational decision but a loving one. The child can rest in their parent's arms and receive whatever they need. That is why the Bible declares that we must come to God as a little child. This is the beginning of an incredible life of faith and as we grow and change, it becomes more dynamic and exciting. We had to learn this first lesson of loving trust all over again as we watched our son slip away from life. We had to make a choice. We can rest in our

Heavenly Father's arms and trust him, or we can torment ourselves by asking over and over again, the three dumbest questions on earth.

They are;
1. Why?
2. Why me?
3. Why me God?

I have seen people who have suffered loss spend the rest of their lives asking these three same unanswerable questions. In fact they still keep coming back into my mind every so often. They are questions that I naturally want answered, and it seems reasonable to ask them. The only problem is that they cause me to lean on my own understanding and consequently stop trusting in the unfailing love of God. Every so often I still find myself asking one of these questions again. Why did this happen to us? Why did God allow it? I have no answer to these questions because eternity and the unseen world cannot be answered from my natural mind. My reason and logic are given to me to understand this created world, not to give me answers about eternity, my destiny, or the spiritual world.

> *We must understand and accept eternity and God by faith*

For these answers I must turn to the creator of the universe in faith and choose to keep trusting in His unfailing love forever. To be honest when I lean on my understanding I actually think God has been incredibly unfair to our family. We have endeavoured to serve God all of our lives and have sacrificed often in the ministry, and then He allows something like this to happen!

> The three dumbest questions on earth.
>
> They are;
> * Why?
> * Why me?
> * Why me God?

If I dwell on the unfairness of what has happened, my mind leads me to resent God and want to turn away from Him. In my mind I often struggle to think that God has acted fairly. However it is not my mind that is created to trust God; it is my heart, and I must choose to trust God with all my heart and not lean on my own understanding.

When I was confronted with Andrew's declining situation which I could not understand, I had to deliberately choose to live by the higher law of faith. Faith believes in the invisible God who created all things, and reaches out with a love that trusts in Him. My mind was racing at a million miles an hour with all kinds of thoughts, fears and dreads and yet I knew I could still choose to live by faith. Faith does not ignore all those thoughts as though they are not real, but chooses to focus on God and His unfailing love for me.

Each dreadful moment I had to choose to believe in the love of God toward me even though I certainly did not feel like it. I am created to love God with all my heart, but unfortunately have been raised to interpret love in tangibly seen and felt actions. This flawed view of love can hinder us from believing in God's pure unconditional love. I had to make a choice to believe in a God who loves me completely. In faith I accept that God created me to enjoy His love and that this broken selfish world is not His fault. I choose to believe in a God who loves me unconditionally. This choice may not change everything I see, but it certainly changes me.

God has created me with the ability to reach out to Him in faith and it all begins by choosing to believe in His unfailing love toward me. I do not understand how it works when everything around me is falling apart, I just trust God that He will never do anything to harm me. He always works everything out for my ultimate good.

During the months of Andrew's sickness I chose to get up early every morning and spend time sitting in my Heavenly father's arms telling Him of my love, and being reassured of His unfailing love for me. It was there in the arms of my Heavenly Father that I learnt how to trust with all my heart. Here are some of the scriptures that helped me trust in God's unfailing love.

Psalm 27:10: "When my father and mother forsake me, then the Lord will take care of me."
LOVE TRUSTS GOD TO NEVER FORSAKE ME.

Psalm 68:5: "A Father to the fatherless, a defender of widows is God in His holy habitation."
LOVE TRUSTS GOD TO BE MY DEFENDER.

Proverbs 3:12: "For whom the Lord loves He corrects, just as a father the son in whom he delights."
LOVE TRUSTS GOD NEVER TO HURT ME.

Isaiah 9:6: "For unto us a child is born, unto us a son is given; and the government will be upon His shoulder. And His name will be called Wonderful, Counsellor, Mighty God, Everlasting Father, Prince of Peace."
LOVE TRUSTS GOD TO BE MY EVERLASTING FATHER.

Matthew 6:8: "Therefore do not be like them, for your Father knows the things you have need of before you ask Him."
LOVE TRUSTS GOD FOR ALL MY NEEDS

> *Faith does not ignore all those thoughts as though they are not real, but chooses to focus on God and His unfailing love for me.*

Matthew 6:32: *"Look at the birds of the air, for they neither sow nor reap nor gather into barns; yet your Heavenly Father feeds them. Are you not of more value than they?"*
LOVE TRUSTS THE VALUE GOD GIVES TO ME.

Matthew 6:32: *"For after all these things the Gentiles seek. For your Heavenly Father knows that you need all these things."*
LOVE TRUSTS GOD IN ALL THINGS

I had to get this foundation of my life in right order. Without the foundation of LOVE THAT TRUSTS being strong, we struggled to live a life of real faith. When we kept this foundation strong we knew we could believe in Him for anything in life and that He loves us unconditionally.

Once this foundation of LOVE THAT TRUSTS becomes a reality, you then begin to experience what it really means to be seated in Heavenly places in Christ. It is not an imaginary place, or a spiritual phrase used in the Bible. Heavenly places became very real to us during our journey through the valley of shadows. I learnt that you can be walking through a place of difficulty, weariness and sorrow, but on the inside you can be at rest and assured that God is in control of all things. In the worst season of our lives, I actually heard myself saying at various times that this was the best season of my life. That defies logic! I don't understand it but I knew God had drawn me closer to Himself and it felt good to live there.

I found God in a greater way and His love became so much more real. God also began to show me that I have to trust Him to lift me up above my broken world of sickness and sorrow. I needed to learn how to trust Him to bring me into a position of rest that looks down from His throne above the brokenness of this natural world.

It sounds great but it is not that easy to achieve. Somehow I had to allow my inner person where God dwells to be lifted up on eagle's wings, while my natural person still walked through the dust of my broken world.

Here is a scripture that helped me get a handle on what these heavenly places are all about.

Ephesians 2:6:
"And raised us up together, and made us sit together in the heavenly places in Christ Jesus."

I started to see it a little clearer. We have the privilege of being able to sit with Christ in the Father's love. Everything feels better when we are at rest in God's royal places. During the whole ordeal with Andrew's sickness, I came to realise all over again the powerful position we have been exalted into with Christ. Jesus Christ has lifted me above the sorrows and restrictions of this earthly world and I can know the incredible joy of sharing a position at the right hand of God the Father through His Son Jesus.

This is a position of rest and refreshing and it became to me a position of quiet confidence. This position of rest in heavenly places is all through the Bible and again when I searched out the scriptures I was challenged to learn how to experience this position of rest.

Matthew 11:28:
"Come to me, all you who labour and are heavy laden, and I will give you rest."

Psalm 37:7:
"Rest in the Lord and wait patiently for Him."

Psalm 110:1:
"The Lord said to my Lord, Sit at my right hand, till I make your enemies your footstool."

Matthew 25:33:
"And He will set His sheep on His right hand, but the goats on the left hand."

Come to me! I would hear the Lord say this to me over and over again. Stop worrying and rest. Stop striving and relax. Stop carrying life like a heavy burden and give it to me.

Hey! When everything is out of control and nothing makes sense anymore, just find a quiet place and sit in the Father's love for a while. Don't ask dumb questions; just relax and let your Heavenly Father love up on you for a while. Remember, He knows every tear we have cried, every sigh we have made, every ache in our body and every desire of our heart. He knows us very well. LOVE THAT TRUSTS gets to know Him very well. And when we do, we will find He is for us not against us. He loves us unconditionally.

Another reason why we must learn to sit in the Father's love and rest in Him; is because it is in rest that we receive revelation from God. God really wants to communicate with us and show us His love. We are often so worried, anxious or just plain busy, that we cannot receive the signals from His heart. We must learn to rest in Him so He can show us His loving-kindness.

There were some days on our journey as we visited the hospital, carried out our ministry duties in the church, and built a new house, that we just became too busy.

> Stop carrying
> life like a heavy
> burden and
> give it to me.

It was then that I realised that the loudest voice in my life was my natural mind. When I moved away from the rest of God's presence my natural circumstances would demand my attention and I would give it to them. I stopped hearing Him say how much He loved me, and soon the cacophony of busy sounds began to dull my senses to God and His wonderful world. It was then I made a fresh commitment to rise early each morning to meet with my loving Heavenly Father.

As I spent time in God's presence I realised that He had prepared a plan for my life from before time began. Way back in eternity before the world was created God knew about our family. He knew about Andrew and our journey through this season of sickness. He knew about everything we would experience in life. He is not taken by surprise by anything that happens in my life.

I found a scripture in Matthew that again helped me to see that God knows about these things before they happen.

Matthew 25:34:
"The King will say to those on His right hand, Come, you blessed of My Father, inherit the Kingdom prepared for you from the foundation of the world."

I could see that God had prepared a wonderful plan for my life from before time began. He loves me and wants to fulfill His plan in my life. To do so means that He must reveal His plan to me through revelation. When I get stressed, worried, anxious, depressed, in turmoil, busy etc. I am not in a position of rest to hear from God. Time after time in the early hours of the morning God would speak to me on the inside, reassuring me that His ways are perfect. He is in control of all things and I do not have to worry about the outcome.

Another strange thing happened when I started to receive revelation from God. I found myself beginning to sing and rejoice. This did not seem possible in light of our natural circumstances as we had absolutely nothing to sing about. On the surface everything looked morbid and depressing. But as I started to receive revelation from God, something inside me started to come to life. I was awakening to the love of God on the inside and it was at first quite confusing, because I was not supposed to be happy in such a sad season.

Our good friends Brian and Bobbie Houston, Senior Pastors of the Hillsong church in Sydney Australia, sent us a pack of their latest worship CD's and these became our songs on the journey through this dark valley. So powerful were these songs that I would often wake up in the night with one of these worship songs stirring in my heart and so would get up and meet with my loving Heavenly Father again in the early hours. Some people did not understand us because we didn't fall into a heap, and they kept telling us it is okay to be sad and fall apart. Sure, there were days when we fell into a heap and let our feelings get the better of us, but we just knew we had to get up again and keep believing that the God who loved us was able to sustain and strengthen us.

We must learn to rest in Him so He can show us His loving-kindness.

I had to keep saying to people over and over again. This is not an act. I actually do feel okay and I do feel like being in church and preaching and rejoicing etc. Resting in the Father's love and receiving revelation is our right as God's children. You don't have to earn it or perform for it. We can

> *But as I started to receive revelation from God, something inside me started to come to life.*

come to Him anytime, even when we are weak and struggling with life's cares and He will give us rest. Supernatural rest! Rest that refreshes and strengthens us to continue on in the journey of faith!

As strange as it may seem, we found a song to sing in the shadows. I found great inspiration and joy as I learned to rest in the Father's love and sit with Him above all my problems, in heavenly places. I also found a whole lot more scriptures as I searched the Bible for meaning and help. The following scriptures all helped me to see that in God's presence can be overflowing joy. I looked for this every day of our journey and on many days it was amazingly present.

Psalm 16:11:
"You will show me the path of life; in your presence is fullness of joy; at your right hand are pleasures forevermore."

Psalm 118:15:
"The voice of rejoicing and salvation is in the tents of the righteous; the right hand of the Lord does valiantly."

Psalm 2:4:
"He who sits in the heavens shall laugh; The Lord shall hold them in derision."

> Love that
> trusts equals
> rest and
> rejoicing.

Luke 6:21:
"Blessed are you who hunger now, for you shall be filled. Blessed are you who weep now, for you shall laugh."

Nehemiah 8:10:
"Do not sorrow, for the joy of the Lord is your strength."

Zephaniah 3:17:
"The Lord your God in your midst, the Mighty One, will save; He will rejoice over you with gladness, He will quiet you with His love, He will rejoice over you with singing."

What amazing scriptures. God gave me rest and rejoicing as I chose to come and sit in His love. This was not an escape for me because I was a weak emotional person needing a crutch. This was one of the hardest and strongest decisions I have ever made in my life. Naturally my reasoning said that I needed sleep and that my prayers were not working, but I chose to trust God above all else. Love that trusts equals rest and rejoicing.

Did we still have times of doubt and uncertainty? Of course! Our human minds would sometimes race out of control and sleep would be impossible. Many nights Marion and I would lie awake, unable to sleep as wave after wave of morbid fear and dread would attack our minds. Marion would often say in the middle of the night, "I need you to hold me for a while."

So we would just lie together, knowing that words were often useless, yet needing reassurance from one another that our steps are ordered by a loving God. I remember lying awake one night being hard on myself for not being stronger and more in control. It was tormenting. I began to allow these thoughts to take over. "I am not making it. I am losing control.

> The Lord shared with me that I do not have to be strong and in control, that is His job

This thing is bigger than I am." It was a wretched night of guilt and self condemnation and I tossed and turned, my bed soaked with sweat until I arose in the early morning hours.

It was that morning, as I came into God's presence to read my Bible and pray, that the Lord shared with me that I do not have to be strong and in control, that is His job. My job is to make sure I enter into His rest and learn to relax in Him. He will cover me with His love if I will come and sit with Him for a while. From that morning on, my rest times with Him became more precious than any other thing.

CHAPTER EIGHT

HOPE THAT BELIEVES

THE EARLY HOURS

The sound of horses shaking off the shadows of the night
And birds beginning their morning rituals of song
The first rays of a sun eager to search out the new day
Await my soul in the early hours

The smell of coffee bubbling with anticipation
in the brewing pot
And the chill of the morning air as it beckons the daybreak
The sound of wind echoing its thoughts
through swaying trees
Await my soul in the early hours

The chair in the corner beckoning as a
familiar place of refuge
And the ageless book so worn yet ever so alive and new
The voice of one who never sleeps yet who greets so eagerly
Await my soul in the early hours

The words of wisdom so deep and so inspiring to my soul
And thoughts of love not able to be expressed in mortal words
The strength and power imparted to my life for
service yet to come
Await my soul in the early hours.

Steve Penny May 2003

Andrew's sickness and death has been the most profound challenge I have ever faced in my life. It has forced me to grow up in many areas of my life and to actually face up to the responsibility for who I am and what I can do in life.

I realised that I had to get up and live life in faith, making sure I had established love as the foundation of my faith, and then to move on and grow in faith. My foundation for everything is a love that trusts God in every area of my life, but now my position of faith had to change. I knew that I could not just sit on God's lap forever expecting Him to work everything out. This would be taking a very fatalistic view of life and I would be abdicating from any sense of partnership with God concerning my destiny. I just knew that I had to do more than say "God's will be done." Sure, I trusted Him to work it all out, but now God was saying that He wanted to work it all out through me. This was to become a great challenge for me. I had to step out in confidence knowing that God loved me and that He promised to work through me. I knew I had to get my mind around this new challenge. God wanted to use me to do His will in this circumstance. There are no hidden areas or special clauses, just an absolute confidence that God loves me and will always be there for me. It is not that I understand why he loves me or how He is always there for me, it is just a decision that even when I don't understand or feel or know it, I will trust.

Once we have learned to rest in His love, and we are comfortable there, the Lord will then gently nudge us that it is time to stand up into the fullness of Christ. And so enters the second part of our trinity of faith.

IT IS TIME TO STAND UP IN CHRIST
I knew I couldn't stay seated in the Father's arms forever. Part of the purpose of me being seated in the love of our heavenly Father is so that I can begin to realise how big God really is. But now He wanted me to stand up in Christ and begin to

> *He wanted me to stand up in Christ and begin to learn how big I am in Him.*

learn how big I am in Him. I couldn't stay seated passively in His love forever! There is a walk of faith to enjoy and fulfill while on planet earth, and so I knew that this whole challenge in our lives was to help me stand up in Christ so I could then grow in confidence to walk in the power of God's Spirit.

Consider the example of a little child again. As the child grows out of the baby stage its loving parents encourage the child to stand up. As strength comes into those little legs so does a confidence that one day the little child will be walking just like other children. The baby must learn to stand before it can walk.

So I knew something was going on in my life to help me fulfill my destiny and serve my creator in a meaningful way. Learning to grow in faith through the three stages of life was going to be quite a journey. I saw that I had to learn to sit as a child, stand as a young person, then finally walk as a grown mature adult. Then I can live in the image of God and fulfill His plan for our lives.

Let me show you again how this trinity of faith works together for good.

LOVE TRUSTS   SIT - in the Father's love
HOPE BELIEVES   STAND - in the fullness of Christ
FAITH ACTS   WALK - in the power of the Spirit

I desperately wanted to make a decision to stand up in Christ and grow into His fullness and I knew that God would not allow me to stay at my present level on His knee forever. The feelings of security comfort and strength, that fill our lives when we are in the presence of God, make it very hard to leave this position of faith and enter the real world where promises must be possessed and battles fought. I would love to stay resting in His love forever, but I knew that it was absolutely essential that I stand up and become more Christ-like if ever I was to fulfill God's purpose for my life on planet earth. This was perhaps the greatest challenge I have ever faced as a Christian. I have never found it hard to believe in God and His awesome ability, but I do struggle at times to believe in my awesome ability in God.

My greatest challenge throughout Andrew's sickness was to stand up and believe that God was with me, and that He wanted me to create a world of possibility by hoping and believing. I found as I learnt this lesson I was being liberated to believe that I could actually change the world I lived in. I could express a hope that believes, and begin to change the world where I live, into a place of expectation and faith.

Again I began to search for scriptures in the Bible that supported this expression of my growing faith and I found so many references to help me build a world of hope wherever I am. I knew this hope had the potential to change everything in my life.

Let me share with you some of the things that the Bible says that hope can accomplish in our lives.

HOPE CREATES AN ENVIRONMENT OF CONFIDENT EXPECTATION

Philippians 1:20:
"According to my earnest expectation and hope that in nothing shall be ashamed, but with all boldness, as always, so now also Christ will be magnified in my body, whether in life or by death."

Hope is the breeding ground of faith

Acts 3:5:
"So he gave them his attention, expecting to receive something from them."

Hope is the breeding ground of faith. As Marion and I drove an hour and a half to the hospital every day, we did everything possible to have hope. We wanted to create a climate and culture of possibility in which our faith could grow and ultimately act. Hope does not just come like a mist and settle on us. We must do something. We had to create a climate and culture of confident expectation that something good can happen even in the midst of dark and hopeless valleys.

We chose to believe that we were on a journey of faith into the blessings of God and there was no need to be ashamed in anything. We were creating a culture of confidence. We could not afford to just sit in the arms of our loving heavenly father, dreaming of the potential of what could be; we had to stand up in Christ and take responsibility to create a world of positive hope that believes.

It is often when difficulty strikes that we attempt to take leaps of faith, only to realise that we have not created a positive environment of hope in which our faith can grow and flourish. It is better to take a stand now and start to create a culture of confidence. We must not live as a "no-hoper." We are to create hope that believes for good things to come into our world. A "no-hoper" is a person who does not see that any good can possibly come out of their present circumstance. I practiced so hard at creating a culture of confident believing so that whenever we went into the hospital and a faith step was required, we would not respond in fear and be

> Create a culture of believing in hope and you will have faith to act when you need it.

immobilised. Fear is the opposite of faith, and both faith and fear are the fruit of the climate and culture we create. Create a culture of believing in hope and you will have faith to act when you need it. Create a culture of doubt and unbelief and you will have fear at work to stop you taking steps of faith.

HOPE BELIEVES FOR THE UNSEEN

Some days we just sat and looked at Andrew's dying body and no matter how hard we prayed it was impossible to have strong faith. We were looking at the natural evidence before our eyes and believing what we saw. Whenever we looked at Andrew's wasting body it significantly weakened our faith.

However beyond the realm of our present reality, is an amazing world of the supernatural kingdom of God. When we create a culture of confident expectation (through hope that believes), we bring these unseen miracles ever closer to manifestation.

One of our most treasured memories of the whole journey was a note Andrew wrote to Marion and I during the early days of his sickness. It was an answer to our prayers and was the fulfilment of all that we believed to see come into reality. Here is the note;

Dear Mum and Dad,

This is just a short note to let you guys know how much Anna and I love you. Your time, care and un-conditional love have been a blessing that have made the first few weeks of this ordeal, bearable. I look forward to sharing many great nights and days as a healthy man serving God with you – and swimming in the pool in your new house. I have always considered you guys my best friends and heroes. I know God has brought this challenge to me to re-focus my life and even though the devil may think he has made in-roads, all he's done is make me more determined to find God's purpose for my life and follow it with all my passion. Let's make God famous and Kings a beacon for Christ in this nation and beyond.

Love Andrew and Anna

Andrew's note was a real shot in the arm for my faith. It was the evidence of what I had believed to see. It was a marvellous insight into the desires of Andrew's heart and I knew that all things do work together for good. The things I had hoped and believed for were now becoming a reality before my eyes.

These following scriptures reveal that it is by hope that we believe to bring into present reality those things that are not yet seen with the natural eye. We are to declare what we have seen in faith, and believe for these things to become present reality in our lives.

John 3:15:
"That whoever believes in Him should not perish but have eternal life."

> You must never
> be ashamed
> because you
> believe; or have
> believed
> in hope.

Romans 8:24:
"For we are saved in this hope, but hope that is seen is not hope; for why does one still hope for what he sees?"

Romans 8:25:
"But if we hope for what we do not see, we eagerly wait for it with perseverance."

Ephesians 1:18:
"The eyes of your understanding being enlightened; that you may know what is the hope of His calling, what are the riches of the glory of His inheritance in the saints."

I had to believe the truth of these scriptures and not the evidence of all the natural circumstances before me. Andrew's body was wasting away, but our hope in God was increasing. Hope perseveres and never stops believing for the good things of God to become present reality. That is why the Bible says that, "hope does not make you ashamed."

You must never be ashamed because you believe; or have believed in hope. There were other days when we would sit by Andrew's side and speak about the times ahead when we would again be playing golf and enjoying the beach. We were trying to create an environment of hope which believed for better outcomes than those being predicted by the doctors.

As I mentioned previously, I had some people come up to me after our son died and say, "We really feel sorry for you, we know how hard you hung on and believed in hope."

I am not ashamed to have hoped in God.

> *I am not ashamed that in my world all things work together for good because I love God and He loves me.*

I am not ashamed to have hung on to every promise of God I could find.

I am not ashamed of every prayer we prayed.

I am not ashamed because I live continually in a culture of hope that believes for good things to come to me from a good God.

I am not ashamed that in my world all things work together for good because I love God and He loves me.

HOPE OVERCOMES DISCOURAGEMENT

Whenever one of the specialists would come into Andrew's room and dump another bad report on us, it would present us again with the opportunity to become discouraged, and on some of these occasions we did allow discouragement to invade our souls and strip us of inner strength. Discouragement is one of the greatest enemies of the human soul.

We are created by God to achieve amazing things in life, and it is often difficult to reconcile apparent failure within this world of hope and believing. Many people try to have extreme faith and will not recognise anything that is less than perfect. Unfortunately all we have to do is give life some time and imperfection will come our way. It is then that we need to learn to overcome discouragement and continue to create this world of hope in God.

> *Hope helps your soul look for answers, not problems.*

Psalm 42:11:
"Why are you cast down, O my soul? And why are you troubled within me? Hope in God; for I shall yet praise Him, the help of my countenance and my God."

I remember having to rush out of Andrew's room on one occasion and get myself back on track, as I had allowed myself to become negative about so many things happening in the hospital at the time. I went into an empty office and just sat down and had a chat with myself about my attitude.

Sometimes you have to give yourself a good talking to about your attitude to life. The Psalmist realised he had become discouraged and that he was disturbed on the inside, and he decided he must change his attitude now. So he began to talk to his soul. Stop being depressed! Stop worrying! Stop keeping me up at night! Stop having a sad facial expression! Start hoping in God! Start believing for a good outcome! Start expecting things to get better! These are the kind of chats that can turn a person's life around. We found that we had to start praising God in our circumstance and it was one of the factors that helped our countenance to change. We knew that if we let discouragement and depression enter our lives it would be so hard to get it out. Marion used to simply look for things to laugh about to keep her soul from being discouraged. Hope helps your soul look for answers, not problems.

The Psalmist began to build a world of hope around him and pretty soon a solution to his dilemma appeared. He created an environment where solutions could surface. This is how hope conquers discouragement. It looks for an answer – which brings encouragement. We sure did look for answers. Marion spent countless hours on the internet searching out every possible remedy for cancer. Some things we tried and some we didn't, but the search for solutions definitely continued to give us hope. It sometimes seems a lot easier to walk around being depressed and discouraged, than to take personal responsibility to change our world and stand up in Christ. Worry and anxiety never helped anyone get anything (other than ulcers!). Hope that believes always helps us look for better things.

HOPE STRENGTHENS YOUR HEART

There came a point when Andrew's health was declining fairly quickly, and it dawned on me that even though Andrew appeared to be dying, I wasn't. I was still very much alive and full of hope. I still had hope to believe for a miracle and suddenly my heart felt stronger and my faith more real than ever before. This is how hope strengthens your heart. It helps you to trust God in everything.

Psalm 31:24:
"Be of good courage, and He shall strengthen your heart, all you who hope in the Lord."

Psalm 27:13:
"I would have lost heart, unless I had believed that I would see the goodness of the Lord in the land of the living."

When we have a hope that believes, we find that our heart starts getting stronger. Don't forget that our heart is our love machine, and so our trust in God gets stronger as

The more we hope and believe in God's goodness, the more our love and trust in Him grows.

-115-

> God has prepared a great place for me in life, but first he must prepare me for that great place.

we continue to hope and believe for good things. If we can keep creating a positive environment of hope, and believe for positive outcomes, we will find our love for God increases and our ability to trust Him is strengthened. So now we can see that the trinity of faith is working together to make us stronger as we grow in faith. Amazing, but true! The more we hope and believe in God's goodness, the more our love and trust in Him grows.

HOPE MAKES YOU INTO SOMEONE

Romans 4:18:
"Against all hope, Abraham in hope believed, and so he became..."

Probably the most powerful comment I have received since Andrew died has been from a friend in ministry. He said, "Steve, you have changed for the better through your ordeal and your preaching since then has gone to a whole new level." I have become a different person. I have changed for the better.

Abraham is one of the great Old Testament heroes of the Bible, who became somebody because he believed in hope. It was the making of him. God promised Abraham that He would give Him two amazing things if Abraham would follow Him in faith. God promised him a land overflowing with every good thing as his inheritance, and also that his seed would become a great nation. However Abraham had to embark on his personal "journey of faith" and choose to follow God, not knowing what the final outcome would be. In fact Abraham had to learn to believe God and hope for the impossible, even when naturally there was no hope of the desired outcome. It was on his "journey of faith", that Abraham became a different person.

God has prepared a great place for me in life, but first he must prepare me for that great place. He wants me to become somebody. I used to believe that if I could pull off some feat of faith I would be a hero. I remember when I first began as a minister praying earnestly for God to help me produce a great miracle in someone's life. I just knew that it would create a real stir and our church would grow overnight. I didn't realise that God had to grow me first before He could grow His church through me. I had to learn to believe God and create a culture of confident expectation before God could give me other people who needed to know how to believe. As we learnt to believe in hope then we began to see miracles happening in our lives. God makes me into someone as I grow in Christ and create my world of confident expectation and hope. I do not become someone by pulling off some great feat of faith, but rather I become someone as I grow in my trust and confidence in God. It is as I develop in confidence that anything is possible with God on my side. This is the part of faith that makes me into someone. Hope believes I am big in Christ. I start to believe that I am able to represent the God I serve. I develop a very healthy self image because I have settled the issue that God loves me and that He wants me to prosper and be successful in all things.

> God makes me into someone as I grow in Christ and create my world of confident expectation and hope.

> The words that we speak are actually our thoughts from within, clothed with the sounds of either our fear or faith.

I knew God had made me into someone the day I stood to speak at Andrew's funeral. I had come a long way in my understanding of God's love for me and I was able to speak to the assembled crowd with authority and confidence that God had everything under control. It is a great feeling to know that God is with us and that we can accomplish great things for Him throughout our lives.

Philippians 4:13:
"I can do all things through Christ who strengthens me."

We must take responsibility for the world we have created. Just as God spoke words to form the original creation, so we have formed the world we live in by the words we have spoken so far. The words that we speak are actually our thoughts from within, clothed with the sounds of either our fear or faith. These sounds have the ability to accomplish our inner desires. When we speak, we release powerful servants to go into our world and perform our will. Our words create our world. We speak into reality the building blocks of our present world. If we speak words of fear and doubt we will create a world of pessimism, discouragement and unbelief. If we speak words of faith and hope – positive words, we will create a world of possibility and expectation.

Some days in the hospital when all appeared lost I would just grit my teeth and make up my mind to become someone by speaking words of hope and expectation. It was extremely difficult on some of our dark days, but as we persisted, pretty soon it felt like we were back living in a world where miracles can happen. My circumstance didn't change but I did. I have

> We refused to let our world be governed by a circumstance.

discovered that as I continue to speak confident, positive, hope filled words, not only will my world change around me, but I will become someone whom God can use.

As Andrew's illness progressed and hope seemed to fade, we realised that we must take responsibility for the world we chose to live in. We were witnessing the decline in Andrew's body right before our eyes. In the natural, it appeared as though all hope was fading. We just knew we had to keep our world of hope alive. We could allow our world to become bleak, depressing and hopeless, or we could in the face of impossibility, continue to speak words of faith and hope, expecting God to still perform a miracle.

Even though we did not see the miracle in the form we were expecting, another miracle was happening. We were becoming different people. Not bitter, sorrowful, fearful and depressed; but stronger, more assured of God, confident that all things do work together for good. We have become better people for the journey because we refused to let our world be governed by a circumstance. We chose to be the creators of our world by continuing to speak and believe words of hope. We became far bigger and better people as we realised that even the worst possible outcomes in our natural world could not destroy our faith in God nor who we had become in Him.

HOPE IS NOT BASED ON PERFORMANCE.

There were many times during our eight month ordeal that we came to the place where we didn't feel as though we could keep going and perform as we should. At one point it all came to a head for me and I just felt as though I had failed God and my family. It was at the end of June and we had not seen the breakthrough that I had confidently told everyone would happen. I began to blame myself for not praying as much as I should and for not being as strong as I felt I should be. It was only after reading the following scripture on hope that I realised that my hope is not based on my ability to be perfect or to perform continually at the highest level. My hope is based on God and His promises toward me.

Ezra 10:2:
"And Shechaniah the son of Jehiel, one of the sons of Elam, spoke up and said to Ezra, "We have trespassed against our God, and have taken pagan wives from the peoples of the land; yet now there is hope in Israel in spite of this."

The above verse is a snapshot of a situation in the history of God's people - Israel. They had disobeyed the commandments of God and had intermarried with nations that God had expressly told them not to intermingle with. The Priest declared that although they had performed badly, there was still hope for them because of God's unfailing love for His people. I love the fact that there is still hope in spite of everything that has happened. This is the power of Godly hope. It is based on God's intention to bless his children no matter what happens. Shechaniah, in the verse above, has caught hold of this truth that there is always hope no matter how poorly you perform. God's grace is always available without conditions and without measure. Often when we perform badly in life, we carry a load of guilt that stops us from receiving God's grace. Once we accept that we have failed in some way and grief takes control, we lose hope of a better day and life becomes a

> *God's grace is simply His provision to enable us to fulfill His plan.*

series of survival drills. This is not the place to live life as God has a far better plan for you.

One of the enemy's greatest weapons is to destroy hope by accusing us that we have not performed well enough for God to act on our behalf. Throughout Andrew's sickness, there were times when I struggled with condemnation because the devil kept whispering in my ear that I wasn't fasting and praying enough.

And so for a while I just tried harder and harder, until I became unwell and exhausted. Then I began to realise that you can never perform well enough. That is why God's grace is available and miracles still happen. God's grace is simply His provision to enable us to fulfill His plan. In spite of our best or worst efforts, there is still hope. God loves us as His children and we are all very special to Him. He will act on our behalf even when we perform badly. And the truth is, we all perform badly at times when put into difficult circumstances.

I knew I had to keep believing in hope. There is nothing I can do that will disqualify me from the love of God. Hope keeps on believing in the love and grace of our God until His plan is perfected in our life. God's plan is always to bless and increase us in all things. Hope never stops believing this no matter what happens. In spite of my flaws, fears and failures, I can still have hope to believe.

> *Hope is the first evidence that I believe a promise of better things.*

HOPE BELIEVES THE WORD – AND STANDS ON IT.

I am absolutely convinced that without God's word for me to stand on during Andrew's sickness and death, I would be a real mess by now. I put together a folder full

> *Hope comes from believing God's word in your heart.*

of scriptures relating to healing and health and overcoming in life, and I used to hold these up in front of Andrew so he could read them. Sometimes he was so sick all he would do is smile and nod his head in agreement. However the promises were doing me a whole lot of good and as I read them they were causing me to hang on to God with a hope that believed.

Psalm 119:49:
"Remember the word to your servant, upon which you have caused me to hope."

Hope is the first evidence that I believe a promise of better things. If I promise to help someone and they believe me, then it produces hope in them that I will perform as promised. God's word is the record of God's promises to us, His children. Sadly many people read the Bible as a book of rules, regulations and punishments. In so doing they miss the whole purpose of God giving us a "book of promises." The Bible is to teach us how to love and trust God. I find the Bible to be the most amazing compilation of incredible promises, and the more I read it the more I am filled with hope of a great future. Because it is God's word, it is infallible, and I can stand on the promises of God and stake my future on them.

Remember! Your hope is based upon the word of God. Hope comes from believing God's word in your heart. Now let me share something that has really helped me to understand the power of God's word in my life of faith. The word of God can be in three places in your life.

> We looked into
> our inner world
> and found
> promises that
> we had
> embraced over
> a lifetime of
> living by faith.

Romans 10:8:
"The word is near you, in your heart and in your mouth, that is, the word of faith which we speak."

THE WORD IS NEAR YOU

Firstly the word can come near you. When I hear or read the word of God it is coming near me. It is entering into my world with the potential to change everything in my world. However I still have to choose to do something with the word when it comes near me. I have to do what Abraham did in Hebrews 11:13. He embraced the promises. He took them to heart. He meditated upon the word of God until it lodged within his heart.

THE WORD IS IN YOUR HEART

This is the second place the word of God can be in our life. In your heart!

It is here that the word of God becomes a word of hope. As we embrace God's promises into our heart, they give us hope. Hopeless people are wordless people, living without promises to believe in. How sad for anyone to go through life without a promise to believe in.

After the shock of discovering Andrew had cancer and being told the prognosis was not good, we then decided to find promises that were already in our heart to believe in, and so hope flourished even when things were at their worst. Because we had been reading God's word for years and hiding it in our heart, we found we quickly had hope; and we still have hope. We didn't go running all over the world looking for someone to give us a special word from God. We looked into our inner world and found promises that we had embraced over a lifetime of living by faith. These promises came to life as we confessed them and they then became our foundation of hope.

THE WORD IS IN YOUR MOUTH

This is the third place that God's word must fill. The actions and confessions of our lives! We must take the Word of God that comes near us, and embrace it into our hearts as a Word of Hope. We must then put it into our mouths as a Word of Faith and confess it into and during our challenges. God's word will then work powerfully inside you as well as in the midst of your trial.

Don't wait for bad things to happen. Begin now to consistently hide the word of God within your heart and mind. You will then have many promises to give hope if difficult days come.

Without this sense of hope, I am not sure whether we could have coped with the awfully challenging road we were given to travel. One of the things that happened during our struggle with Andrew's sickness was that we again realised afresh that God's word was our foundation, and to this day it has never let us down. It actually became our reference point for most of what we talked about or thought about.

HOPE BELIEVES YOU ARE BIG IN CHRIST

One of the most liberating revelations that came to me after Andrew died was that I still had a life to live. You see! My son may have died; but I didn't. I am still very much alive and believing for even greater things to happen through my life for His glory. That is what hope does. It makes you into somebody. Whether you win on the stock market or lose your son to cancer, you can know that you are somebody and that

God has a great plan for your life. I know God has great plans for my future, and the death of my son Andrew has not lessened any of these plans. In fact if anything God is increasing my faith to believe that I can possess even more because I have become a bigger person through it all.

Philippians 4:13:
"I can do all things through Christ who strengthens me."

I have been through the worst situation a parent can face; the death of one of our children before our eyes. And yet I am not destroyed by what has happened. It dawned on me that I have conquered one of the worst trials that a man can face. I actually feel like there is very little that could intimidate me in my faith in God from now on. This is the real challenge in life. To stand up in Christ and believe I am able to "do all things through Christ."

If I will build a world of hope that believes, I will soon find myself confidently believing that in Christ I am more than a conqueror. I am convinced that the major challenge in the Christian life is to stand up in Christ and believe I am able to do all things with His help. I must see myself as a big person serving and living for a big God. Hope helps me feel good about myself and my future. It lets me see beyond the mirror of my present circumstance into the possibility of God's promise of a greater future. We had to choose to stop feeling miserable, and start believing for better days and better things to come our way. That's what hope does.

> *This is the real challenge in life. To stand up in Christ and believe I am able to "do all things through Christ."*

HOPE HAS A UNIQUE SOUND

> *People who have learned to create a world of hope seldom stay depressed for long.*

The most annoying sound in the hospital is firstly the sound of the beepers on the machines that dispense all the potions into the body. When a bag of liquid is empty the machine sets off a beeper that can be heard for quite some distance. These beepers can be constantly heard from many rooms as staff hurry from one bed to the next to attach a new bag of liquid. The second most annoying sound in hospital is the sound of patients and friends complaining over the poor service afforded to them. The patients and friends lounge was the perfect place for a disgruntled visitor to offload their pent up feelings on total strangers.

And yet there would be others who would always be positive and bright no matter their lot in life. These were the ones who kept hoping for a better day; who refused to give in or be dragged down by their surroundings. These were the people everyone wanted to talk to. Marion was one of these. Everyone was happy to see Marion as she would always have a word of hope for discouraged patients and friends.

You can always tell people who have a hope that believes. They have a different sound. They have a confident attitude toward life. They have a song in the shadows of life. They can comfort others with words of hope. They have a confident confession that their faith in Christ makes all things possible. They never stop believing and confessing that better things are in store for them.

People who have learnt to create a world of hope seldom stay depressed for long. In fact people who live with hope in their

> Whenever we talk about things that inspire hope, we find that our sound changes, and so does our world.

lives are great people to be around. We can choose to stand up into the fullness of Christ and create a positive world of confidence and hope, or we can choose to simply reflect and describe the circumstances we find ourselves in.

If you can believe that your best days are ahead of you and talk as if they are, you will be amazed at the way your words affect your demeanour and even help lift you out of your present circumstance. We found that many people visiting the patients lounge thought they were expected to describe everything that was wrong in their world. When Marion and I would ask them about the other parts of their world, other than their loved one who was sick, they would light up and begin to talk with a different sound. It all has to do with what you focus on and decide to talk about. Whenever we talk about things that inspire hope, we find that our sound changes, and so does our world.

CHAPTER NINE

FAITH ACTS

THE GOOD REPORT

Like cool breezes sweeping down from the
mountains on a hot summers day
Bringing longed for relief and a pause from the fray
And with its refreshing comes strength to go on
This good report in the night has become
my refuge and my own sweet song

Like words so lovingly and thoughtfully expressed
Revealing true friendships and a companions caress
Each word is a story just longing to be told
This good report on the page keeps on saying
be strong and be bold

Like a hot meal so faithfully delivered to our home after dark
And each dish a delight to warm a weary ones heart
Knowing hands have prepared this expression of love
This good report in a dish pours grace into our
lives from the one up above

Like calls on the phone and the beep of
a new SMS just arrived
Bringing greetings and thoughts from those unable to spend
much time at your side
Yet always the knowledge that they are praying for you
This good report from a distance helps us see life from a very
different view

Steve Penny August 2003

> *God will take responsibility for the outcomes if I will take responsibility for my actions.*

The head specialist had just left Andrew's room after delivering another bad report. It was late in the day and Andrew had had more than enough things go wrong for one day. He told us we should go on home as it was getting late and had been a very flat day.

We started to pack our things and then out of the blue Andrew said, "Hey Dad we need to pray for a better day tomorrow. I don't want another day like today." I was thrilled to hear Andrew speaking so strongly with faith and we all prayed extra hard that night for a real breakthrough the following day. We were all learning how to not only trust God and believe in hope for good things, but now our lessons were focused on how to act in faith expecting to see the things we believed for.

This journey of faith just keeps on demanding that I grow up and take responsibility for my actions. God will take responsibility for the outcomes if I will take responsibility for my actions.

LOVE TRUSTS   SIT - in the Father's love
HOPE BELIEVES   STAND - in th fullness of Christ
FAITH ACTS   WALK - in the power of the Spirit

Every day as we visited Andrew in hospital we had to act on what we hoped for. We hoped for him to be completely healed and so we had to perform actions that would bring about his healing. We would lay our hands on his body and command the cancer to leave and believe for God's healing life to flow into his body. This is acting in faith on what we believed to happen. It is not a difficult decision, nor is it an uncomfortable action. Why? Because we have been building a world of confident believing in which our faith can flourish.

Our faith is not based on some superhuman feat, but on the consistency of God's word in our lives. We knew that we had to be consistently acting out our faith in our everyday activities. We believed Andrew was going to be healed so we spent time planning for holidays with him when he would come home well again. We were acting in faith. It was not a matter of wait and see, but acting out what we believed to see happen. We seamlessly moved from a confident expectation of hope to acting out what was in our heart. As we act and speak according to the word upon which we hope, we have a sense that the time is right to step out in faith. The funny thing about faith is that it is always the right time to step out in faith. This kind of confidence is created by people who believe in hope. An environment of confident hope creates an attitude of now action.

We visited the hospital every day expecting that this would be the day we would see our miracle. As we prayed and laid our hands on Andrew we never once doubted that his miracle was about to happen. We created a culture of confident expectation so that anytime there was a challenge or bad report we were ready to step out in faith. We did not have to fast and pray and wait for some extra special word from God. We were ready and willing to believe God and get on with walking in the power of the Holy Spirit. We were ready to act in faith and prepared to have a go. We refused to be intimidated. We

> *Our faith is not based on some superhuman feat, but on the consistency of God's word in our lives.*

> *The Holy Spirit's role is not to try to get me started in faith, but to guide me as I have a go.*

did whatever we could with what we had. The Holy Spirit's role is not to try to get me started in faith, but to guide me as I have a go.

This acting in faith was the real challenge when we went into the world of sickness and death. Andrew knew what we were doing and joined with us to act as best we could with positive faith. Let me share some of the things I learned that helped us to walk by faith in the power of the Holy Spirit.

FAITH ACTS ON WHAT THE HEART LOVES

Matthew 6:21:
"For where your treasure is, there your heart will be also."

We knew we had to make Andrew's healing our highest priority. We felt at times as though we were neglecting our other children, but we knew they understood. We had to focus our desires and dreams on Andrew's full recovery. This was our top priority!

You will ever only step out in faith to possess what your heart treasures. Faith acts to possess what you make your highest priority. Faith leaps toward what the heart desires and loves. Therefore it is a simple thing to serve God and live by faith when you have taken the time to establish a love that trusts God in everything. Sitting in the Father's love allows you to love what the Father loves, and have faith to possess what the Father says is yours.

FAITH ACTS ON WHAT THE MIND CONCEIVES.

I knew that I had to see Andrew well again in my mind. I had to see him strong again no matter how far off it seemed. It was now time to get my mind into gear and align my thinking with what my heart desired.

You will ever only step out in faith to possess what your heart treasures. Faith acts to possess what you make your highest priority.

Hebrews 11:13:
"These all died in faith, not having received the promises, but having seen them afar off were assured of them, embraced them and confessed that they were strangers and pilgrims on the earth."

Hebrews 11:15:
"And truly if they had called to mind that country from which they had come out, they would have had opportunity to return."

We must see in our mind what we know in our spirit. When confronted with the graphic evidence of sickness, disaster and loss, our mind is filled with every detail of this profoundly distressing evidence. This is what happened to us as we were continually presented with the facts of Andrew's declining health. If we were going to change those circumstances then we had to find the promises of God in our heart and choose to meditate and think upon them until our mind could conceive and believe what our heart knew to be true about God.

We all subconsciously spend time thinking on the things that control our heart. Our thoughts will always return to the things that rule our hearts. They will be either desires for good things or a dread concerning bad things. In our heart (spirit) we form convictions that dominate our thinking (mind).

Have you ever heard someone who finally understands something you are saying declare, "Oh I get it, I can see it!" This is what must happen in our mind because thoughts control our decisions. We must "get it". The promises from God that we know to be true must register in our mind until they dominate our thinking. This only happens through meditation and repeatedly affirming God's promises in our thoughts. There comes a moment when we "get it." It is now in our thinking as a dominant thought and it can from now on, empower our will to give us permission to act that way. Our spirit is for believing, but our mind is for behaving. We must be able to comprehend in our mind what our spirit believes or else we will end up having a spiritual set of convictions but live out of a natural set of behavioural commitments. We knew we had to take time to get our head around what our heart believed. We can never understand life in all its variables except through faith in God and His promises, so we need to determine how our faith in God should act.

> Our thoughts will always return to the things that rule our hearts.

Faith is not blind nor is it dumb. Faith comes alive when we hear God's word twice in our lives. Faith comes from hearing God's word in our heart as a promise, and then hearing it again in our mind as a plan. As we meditate on the promises of God we begin to formulate a plan of action. Faith sees the challenges but chooses to act anyway. Faith realises the consequences and chooses to risk all for a positive outcome.

> *No-one has ever done anything in life except they did it first in their mind.*

Our mind must know what our faith wants to do. Our mind is our permission giver. We say either, "I will or I won't" from our mind, irrespective of what our heart believes. We will never give ourselves permission to act in faith if our mind has not settled on a plan of action. It is therefore very important to only call to mind what we want to act upon. We must never go anywhere in our mind that we do not intend to go in real life. No-one has ever done anything in life except they did it first in their mind.

To dwell on negative thoughts and fears in our mind is to lay a roadmap in our subconscious that we will automatically follow in real life. We must never let our mind dwell on negative thoughts. Just don't go there. Focus on thoughts that help us to act positively concerning any challenge. We learn to give ourselves permission to act in faith by adopting a clear plan of action in our minds. We do this by habitually thinking on positive outcomes.

FAITH ACTS DAILY TO DO GODS WILL

I had to learn to walk by faith every day I was in the hospital. My faith had to be consistent on the good days and the bad days. The whole deal about living by faith is the way we act on a daily basis. I found this scripture that said I had to keep my confidence strong and keep enduring on a daily basis. I knew God was teaching me to make faith a daily journey.

Hebrews 10:35:
"Therefore do not cast away your confidence, which has great reward. For you have need of endurance, so that after you have done the will of God, you may receive the promise."

Taking daily steps of faith is doing the will of God. God in His wisdom has divided our lives into mini "journeys of faith". They are called days, and we have three hundred and sixty five of them in every year of our life. God did this so we could trust Him for our daily resource. The Bible says that His mercies are new and fresh every morning. God programmed us to live a daily life of faith. Faith does not believe for some far off distant miracle to someday drop into your lap. This kind of waiting for some great miracle event to happen is not doing the will of God.

I had no idea how many days we would be bound to our hospital routines, but I came to see that all I had to do was believe God for His grace to be sufficient for the day I was in. Every day was a new day of faith to believe for a miracle. God expects us to daily follow Him and walk by faith in the power of the Holy Spirit. The Bible says that we are to continually be filled with God's Spirit so that we can be empowered to act in faith in the everyday circumstances of life.

DAILY STEPS OF FAITH CAN FAIL

I have never felt as low as I felt when Andrew died. Not only had we lost a wonderful son, but somehow inside it felt like I had failed in my walk of faith. All I knew was that we had lost our son and I didn't know what to do about it except turn to the one I trusted the most. My Heavenly Father! It was when I turned to Him that I found out that everything was okay and that He had everything under control. A couple of scriptures that really explain how we can miss it and fail in our faith walk are as follows;

Luke 22:32:
"But I prayed for you, that your faith should not fail;"

Psalm 37:23:
"The steps of a good man are ordered by the Lord, and He delights in his way. Though he fall (fail in faith) he shall not be utterly cast down; for the Lord upholds him with His hand."

It is possible for us to fail in our daily walk of faith. Most people I know would admit to the fact that not everything they set their hand to succeeds exactly as planned. Andrew's death was far less than my expectation for good; in fact it was the exact opposite of all I had believed for. It seemed absolutely like a failure in faith.

Faith is the positive expectation of the highest outcome for our good and God's plan. When the absolute best outcome does not eventuate it can then be perceived that we have "failed in faith." When I refer to "failures in faith" I am using a term that perhaps we can understand, although I absolutely believe that nothing is a failure when God is at work. All things, the Bible says, will work out for good.

> *Faith is the positive expectation of the highest outcome for our good and God's plan.*

I have had big and small "failures in faith". Things just haven't happened how and when I expected them to. The death of our son Andrew appeared to be a failure in faith. I tried everything I knew in faith and it still didn't happen as I expected. There have been many times when I have prayed for people and have seen God miraculously heal and deliver them, whilst others have just got worse and died. I consider these times when the outcome I expect does not happen, as "failures in faith."

I can see now that it is possible to have "failures" in faith, while not allowing my faith to fail. My faith does not fail when I trust in the Father's love and I surrender to Him what appear to me as "failures in faith." When I live in the trinity of faith I can never fail, even though I may experience apparent "failures in faith."

I will never forget an occasion when it appeared to many as though I had failed in faith. It was early in my ministry when we were building a new church for our growing congregation. We had purchased land and with great excitement had decided to have a church working bee on the property. Many people had come to help clean up the property as well as some trucks with machinery to move some soil to fill in a creek area.

Half way through the morning the sounds of happy people working together were shattered by the roar of someone in terrible agony. It was one of the most chilling sounds I have ever heard. One of the trucks had backed down into the creek to dump a load of soil. The truck was overfilled and as the tray full of soil was raised it started to lean to one side. The driver called to one of our men to reach under the truck and pull a lever to lower the tray down again. This was a makeshift lever as the one in the cabin was not working. Unfortunately the man reached his arm through between the tray and chassis and when he pulled the lever the tray came crashing down shattering his arm from the elbow to the shoulder. Chaos followed with people running everywhere trying to release this man from his awful predicament. Children, shocked by the bloody scene, went running back to their parents

After the ambulance had gone and the family members had been notified, I was sitting on a log watching our people leave quietly to take their shocked children home. As I sat there deeply affected by this awful event, one of the leaders of the church came to me and said the following words, "Steve, this is your fault. You have gone ahead of God and now you have blood on your hands. You will never build this building."

I went home absolutely devastated by the events of the day and by the words my so-called friend had dumped on me. I went through weeks of morbid introspection and doubt before I began to listen to true friends around me who continually encouraged me that God was still with us. I can see now that I was in danger of letting my faith fail, just because I had experienced a "failure of faith" on the journey of faith. We began to encourage each other that God was still in control of our lives and that we would yet build a great church for God. Today that church has gone from strength to strength and is a lighthouse in its city.

I have had many "failures" in my walk of faith over the years but I have come to see that nothing can separate me from the love of God and that He will deliver me from every snare and trap of the enemy. To be honest, the greatest victories of faith I have ever experienced have often come after I have picked myself up following an apparent "failure in faith". The deliberate decision to go on in faith after you have, "messed up or missed it", is one of the greatest decisions you can ever make. Sadly, the pathway of faith is littered with people who have "failed in faith" and refused to get over it, get up, and get on with living for God.

> The deliberate decision to go on in faith after you have, "messed up or missed it", is one of the greatest decisions you can ever make.

Please do not stew in your failure. Do not let guilt or grief tie you down to some failure in faith which is now well in the past.

Sure it didn't happen as we expected but that is where our faith in the living God comes in. He can and will restore to you the joy of your salvation and you can and will go on from strength to strength. All you have to do is know what to do when it appears as though you have "failed in faith."

And so we are about to learn one of the greatest lessons in faith we can ever possibly learn.

THE GREATEST IS LOVE

I lift my head to the one who knows all things
And wonder at your graciousness
In planning my steps with such infinite wisdom
And ordering all things to work together for good
Because of your great love for me
How great your love

You O Lord are an ever present help at all times
Your shadow is my covering and my life
I walk as one who knows no fear
And watch to see your increasing plan
Unfold with absolute precision and blessing
How great your love

I will bless you Lord at all times and give you praise
For you alone have made me to know your love
If I could count my days they would be as dust
Compared to a moment in your presence
Where light and love explode in glorious ways
How great your love.

Steve Penny July 2003

I sat alone after it was all over. Andrew's funeral was over and all our wonderful friends and family had gone home. It felt very strange. It had been a huge day with so many friends coming from near and far. Many of our family and friends from around Australia and overseas, had come to offer their love and support and had added greatly to what turned out to be an inspirational time for us all. But now as I sat at home, feeling so empty and alone, I sensed the presence of God invading my low point. It was as though the Lord was reaching down into my moment of despair and lifting me up ever so gently. I began to realise that God was bathing me in His love. Just like a grandparent spends time helping a little child in a nice warm bath, so God was nourishing my soul in the most amazing way. Something was happening that I couldn't explain. It was like I was being washed from all the sorrow and pain of the day, and I felt so clean and loved and strong again.

I was being drawn back to the place of love again, where I could just sit in the Father's love and be nourished by Him all over again. It was then that I began to get a first glimpse into the revelation as to why love is the greatest. You must see that God's love never fails, and I was about to learn the greatest lesson of my life. Our scripture declares that love is the greatest of these three facets of faith. Let me show you some reasons why.

LOVE CONTINUES TO TRUST WHETHER FAITH WINS OR NOT

After Andrew's death, God took me back to the place of His love and I learned to sit in His love all over again. He showed me that He is in control of all things and that all I had to do was to rest in His love and trust in Him. Our faith can fail in our daily walk for God and not everything is perfect and comes to pass as we expect. It is when we fail in faith that we hear the voice of God say; "Go directly back to love and I will

> *We do not know what the future holds and therefore must love and continually trust the one who holds the future, especially when He pulls rank.*

meet you there." God loved me and restored me to wholeness, and I knew that He was working all things together for His good. When I returned to His love I knew that it was all alright. You see, love continues to trust whether He prospers you or not. Whether He promotes you or not! Whether He performs for you or not! Whether He protects you or not! Whether He heals your son or not! Love continues to trust Him in all things. It was love that sent Jesus to the cross of Calvary. Not just love for a sinful world, but love for His Father in heaven. It was a love that trusted His Father to work all things together for His and our good. That is why love can never fail.

You will have occasions in life when some of your best efforts of faith just do not work out as you expected. In these times there will be those who conclude that your faith has failed. Do not agree with them. You may have "failed in faith", but your faith has not failed. Your faith is a gift from God therefore it cannot fail.

This is not the time to become self conscious and ashamed and retreat back to a safe level in life. Absolutely not! It is a time to run to the Father's love and realise that He is always there and that your faith can never fail when you are in Him.

LOVE CONTINUES TO TRUST WHEN GOD PULLS RANK

Why would God want to play games with our family? Taking our son home to heaven seemed like such a stupid thing to do when he was so young. Again my mind just can't grasp such an impossible action. Surely God could have healed Andrew and it could have all been for His glory. I knew I just had to trust. The following verse from Job kept stirring inside me and I knew it was God talking to me about absolute trust.

Job 13:15:
"Though He slay me, yet will I trust Him."

Sometimes God pulls rank for your greater good. Love trusts God to know best when He pulls rank and does not explain all the details to you. I felt like God pulled rank in our family for reasons I will never understand this side of eternity. But when I returned to the place of love, my heart fully trusted in Him. My head said it was unfair; it should not be this way, but my heart trusted in the one I love, and I just knew He would always do me good.

In fact if I stop to think about what has happened to me I could become very bitter very quickly. Why? Because I am trying to understand eternity with my natural mind! Remember it is your heart that is created to understand eternity, not your mind or head. Do not lean to your understanding, it will kill you. When God pulls rank He has a greater purpose and plan at work and all we can do is trust Him and His unfailing love.

After Andrew's death we received some flowers with a card from some ministry friends in Australia who had also lost a son through an accident some years earlier. They shared a scripture with us that had been an encouragement to them during their time of loss. It became an encouragement to us also. In essence the scripture said, "He delivers the righteous from the evil to come." We do not know what the future

> *God believes the best about you at all times and wants you to always believe the best about His plan for your life.*

holds and therefore must love and continually trust the one who holds the future, especially when He pulls rank.

LOVE BELIEVES THE BEST AT ALL TIMES

At some stage I knew that I would have to believe the best about God and his plan for our family. If I couldn't do this then I knew I would struggle for the rest of my life. God has my best interests at heart and I have to believe the best about God and His intentions for me.

Romans 8:28:
"And we know that all things work together for good to those who love God, to those who are called according to His purpose."

How can everything work out for good when the son you believe will be in the ministry with you is dying before your eyes? It would have been so easy to believe this verse if Andrew had been healed and restored to full health and strength. However Andrew did not live and we had to reconcile this scripture with everything God was saying to us. It did not seem possible until we came back to God in simple faith and said again that we trust in Him.

You cannot help but know that it will all be alright when you sit on your Heavenly Father's knee. Love that trusts knows and believes that all things are working together for good. God believes the best about you at all times and wants you to always believe the best about His plan for your life. When

> *There is no higher force on the planet than God's love toward me and it will never fail.*

you love and trust someone you will always believe the best about them. It was never an issue during Andrew's sickness that God was angry with us or was punishing us for some remote misdeed. Sure, the enemy tried to load us up with guilt over the "bad parent" trip, but we refused to accept this. We knew our Father's love too well to fall for that old ruse. God loved us and was working His perfect will in our lives.

LOVE NEVER FAILS

I have discovered through personal experience that there is no higher force on the planet than God's love toward me and it will never fail.

1 Corinthians 13:8:
"Love never fails."

Love can never fail for love is of God, and God can never fail. This was one of the greatest moments of my life. When I returned to the love of my Heavenly Father, having appeared to have failed in faith, and He said to me, "you haven't failed, for love never fails." At that very moment I realised it is not about the outcome, but the journey. The journey leads into God's presence and into His fullness for my life.

The outcomes of faith belong to the Lord. What God wants from me is a life of faith that continues to grow from strength to strength whether I see the outcomes I expect or not. I began to realise that "in all these things"; both the good times and

> The outcomes
> of faith belong
> to the Lord.

the bad, the love of God will sustain me, and when I continue in His love I can never ever fail. Oh sure, there will be times when it looks to the natural mind as though my attempts at faith have failed, but as soon as I return to the Father's love, I realise all over again, I am still on the winning side, and I still have a great inheritance, and I still have many great victories ahead.

LOVE COVERS ALL OUR MISTAKES

I cannot begin to explain the freedom that came into my soul as I realised that God's love covers every mistake I have ever made. No wonder it is such a great place to run back to after an apparent failure in faith.

During Andrew's sickness there were a number of times when I acted poorly toward God and others who were just trying to help in their own way. Knowing I had made a mistake then produced a sense of condemnation and uncertainty as to whether I could continue to believe God for miracles. It was in these times that I learnt to return to the Father's love and find that His love has already covered my sins, and released me from judgment. Confidence flowed again to believe God for awesome things. Look at the following scripture that clearly says that love covers all sins.

Proverbs 10:12:
"Hatred stirs up strife, but love covers all sins."

Even when we make mistakes and fail from the way of our faith, if we will return to His love He is faithful and just to forgive us and to cover our sins with His blood. His love then restores our soul and we begin again to see His great plan for our lives. You must know that God loves you and

> You must know
> that God loves
> you and covers
> all your sins
> and failures
> with His love.

covers all your sins and failures with His love.

LOVE CONQUERS ALL THINGS

Romans 8:37:
"Yet in all these things we are more than conquerors through Him who loved us."

Andrew lay motionless on the bed as the tears flowed down our cheeks and splashed all over the bedclothes. He was dead. The battle was lost and we were absolutely shocked that the end had happened so suddenly. What had been predicted as weeks or even months had happened in just nine days and we did not know what to do next.

The next morning after Andrew had died was a very strange visit into God's presence in the early hours. I had been so focused on staying strong and believing for a miracle that now I struggled to find a purpose for being in God's presence.

However it soon became apparent that God knew what I would be experiencing and I didn't have to say a word. God just loved me and let me rest in Him and find comfort for my sorrow in His presence. I had found my place of refuge after the fight and even though there was some sense of personal failure, I soon found that it was covered by His love and removed from my soul.

Love was the foundation I needed to return to when all else seemed to have failed. Love will never fail. I was being restored and nourished with unbelievable love. Greater love than I could ever imagine possible, and some time later, when I was ready again I heard my Father say to me, "It is time for you to stand up again in my Son and complete the task I sent

> The depth of God's love can only be truly known by those who have returned to Him following some "failure in faith."

Him to perform on earth. You are my servant in whom I am well pleased, stand up and go on with this confidence, that you are wiser and stronger than before." The Father's love allowed me to step out in confidence again knowing that I was more than a conqueror through Him who loved me first. The depth of God's love can only be truly known by those who have returned to Him following some "failure in faith."

I remember returning to Australia after completing my National Service in the army having served in Vietnam as a twenty year old Christian young man. During my time overseas I had turned my back on the God I knew so well and had failed in my faith on many occasions. I was absolutely messed up and very conscious of the fact that it was my own doing and therefore deserving of God's judgment.

I attended a youth camp sometime after I returned to Australia and it was there that God began to show me how much He loved me. Meeting after meeting I sat there crying silently as the speaker preached from God's word. He was not judging or condemning, but sharing on God's great plan for our lives. It was not long before I responded to the invitation to return to the love of God and be restored. It was that night that I experienced God's love in a way I had never thought possible. It was as if waves of liquid love were flowing over me, and it continued for hours after the service had finished. I knew that God was forgiving me and washing me clean, but I also knew that something far greater was also happening. God was embracing me in His love in such a powerful way that it felt

> There is nothing that I have done that takes God by surprise or alienates me from His love.

like I was being enveloped in arms of steel from heaven. It was then that I knew that nothing could ever separate me from the love of God, as long as I would run back to Him after every "failure in faith."

That night at the youth camp became a watershed moment in my life. God showed me why He sent His son Jesus to die for my sins. He showed me that I am created as a son of God and there is nothing He will not do to help me live a life of blessing and victory. His love is His guarantee of eternal life. I cannot earn it nor perform well enough to deserve it. It is because of His amazing love for me that He will go to any lengths to restore me to His plan. God loves me unconditionally. God loves me eternally. God loves me and there is nothing that can separate me from this incredible love. It is mine forever, as long as I decide to live in it and run back to it, if and when I fail in my walk of faith. I experienced these same steel arms from heaven wrapping me up in God's great love after Andrew had died. God was letting me know that I counted in His plan and that He was not finished with me yet.

Since then I have never once doubted God's love for me, nor His ability to restore me and put things right again. There is nothing that I have done that takes God by surprise or alienates me from His love. I decided to run back to my heavenly Father knowing He has created me for His pleasure and He loves me and is waiting to restore me to His love and to my true destiny. I could not stay where I was, but chose to get up and return back to the love of God.

If you are in a position where it looks like you have failed in your faith then do not stay there but get up and run back to the amazing love of God. Ask for His forgiveness and you will get it. Believe for His power to change your life and He will do a miracle in your life. God has given you the great gift of faith and through it you can live forever in His amazing love. And so the trinity of faith continues to work in our lives as we go from strength to strength and from glory to glory.

CHOOSING YOUR REAL WORLD

I see a hand you cannot see which beckons me away
I hear a voice you cannot hear which says I must not stay
I see a city on a hill its light is meant for me
I hear its music and its song so glorious and so free
I cannot stay in this dark place where all has come undone
I choose to live in a different world created by God's son
I see a path I have not trod and know that I must rise
Toward a day with noonday sun and heavens open skies
I'll never be the same again His call becomes so clear
Well done good faithful servant your destiny draws near

Steve Penny June 03

> We had to determine which world we wanted to live in.

Every day when we entered the hospital ward, the special routines would begin. Firstly the washing of our hands with special sterilising stuff. Then the long walk down the corridor toward Andrew's room. As we approached we would strain for any sounds of life, but he was usually bombed out on drugs.

The bedside vigil would then begin. Endless hours staring at a lifeless form, waiting for those brief interludes when he would rally for a while and we could enjoy his company. In the between times there was always the visitors lounge for family and friends. This room became a wonderful haven where we could enjoy a cup of tea or make a piece of toast. Both family and patients would end up in the visitors lounge to watch TV or to attempt to solve a jigsaw puzzle. Others would just sit and talk about the vagaries of their illness and the probabilities of their cures.

It was a dismal hopeless place filled with sad and lonely people. It was a complete eye opener for us. We had entered a different world. One filled with sickness, sorrow and death, and it was drawing us into its web. Before long these sick and lonely people had become our friends. We were walking the same road together and living in the same world. It wasn't long before we noticed that our world had changed and our lives were taking on a whole different perspective. Our language and conversations were different. Our eating places and time schedules had changed. Our routines were now totally different.

What had changed? Sickness had entered our world, and was now attempting to draw us into its world. The world of sickness and disease, sorrow and loss is such a small world. We began to realise that we had a real battle on our hands.

> *I therefore made it my mission to stay in touch with the real world and maintain it as my dominant world.*

We had to determine which world we wanted to live in. Sickness had entered our world, but we had to decide whether the world of sickness would become our future place of residence.

This subtle change in our lives continued to happen until we realised one day that we had become captive to this world of sickness and disease. We had started to define everything in the light of Andrew's sickness and had unconsciously developed routines based on our hospital commitments, and although many of these things were essential we found ourselves responding to people and commitments in our real world in a detached manner. It happens quite naturally when you have a terminally ill or impaired person in your immediate family.

Andrew's cancer had suddenly propelled us into a totally different world. Now we spent most of our days in a hospital ward mixing with the terminally ill. Dying people became our daily social network. Families of dying people engaged us in deep and meaningful conversations. All related to sickness and death. There are very few moments of joy in this deep dark world of sickness and disease.

I was learning a little of what people who have long term impairment have to face on a daily basis. I don't know when it happened but there came a day when I realised that I had been drawn into a world of sickness and disease. I was embroiled in this world, but I knew I didn't have to let it become my real world. I made up my mind that I would enter this world with the express purpose of changing it, not it

> *Visit the world of sickness as often as you want, but do not let it become your world.*

changing me. I refused to spend long hours talking over every possible scenario relating to the sickness, or of every little issue relating to the dismal reports coming from this world. I wanted out, but I couldn't get out because our time in this broken world of sickness was not yet over. I therefore made it my mission to stay in touch with the real world and maintain it as my dominant world.

Marion and I would continually go downstairs to the coffee shop and enjoy a latte, and even get out of the hospital completely and go to a restaurant in the city, to reaffirm that there was still a real world out there. So many people let the world of sickness and despair envelope them into its shroud of darkness and depression; it tells them things are hopeless, and consequently they lose faith to believe for miracles.

We stayed connected to our church. We attended the meetings on the weekend as often as we could. We continued to go forward in life. We built a new house, bought new investment properties and tried to live in the real world of faith, hope and love. We encouraged Anna to stay at work and to maintain her real world involvements and I believe it helped her to get through the most painful time any young wife should ever have to endure. This world of sickness will reduce everything you have and want to be, into a shrivelled up shell of despair and grief.

> *Never reduce your real world down to the size of the devil's world. He lives at the lowest level and we are called to live at the highest level.*

IT IS A RESTRICTING WORLD

This world of sickness and disease restricts everything you do. Your life is not your own any longer. You are restricted in your freedoms as many other demands are now being made of you. I found myself being restricted to routines that were completely foreign to me.

You must not let this world of sickness and disease restrict who you are and what you can do. Make every effort to stay in your real world which has future dreams and hopes, and maintain your freedoms of being able to go out with friends and enjoy some of the little pleasures of life. Visit the world of sickness as often as you want, but do not let it become your world.

Have you noticed how quiet you have to be around sick people? How sad you must look and serious you must be? I never realised the restricting boundaries that are placed upon you when you visit a hospital ward. Something inside me wanted to scream out that I didn't belong here and I wouldn't give in to their demands. When did this world take over? Who said you have to lose your joy because someone you love is sick? Who said you must speak in serious undertones around sick people? I actually found that we needed to bring our happy joyful world into Andrew's ward and bring him into contact with the real world.

IT IS A REDUCING WORLD

This world of sickness and disease reduces everything down to the lowest level. Your finances are reduced. Your time is reduced. Your mobility is reduced. You will ultimately be reduced to being a spectator of decline and reduction in every area. That is why Jesus said that the devil comes to steal, kill and destroy. Jesus spoke this about the devil as a comparison to His own plan to bring life to its fullest for everyone who would believe in Him. The devil went from the highest place in creation –next to the throne of God – to the lowest place in creation. His plan now is to reduce every person created in the image of God to his low level world. He will do this through any means possible. Jesus has come to planet earth to lift up a broken humanity and restore us to the highest place next to God's throne. No wonder the devil hates you. You are destined to fill his place next to the throne of God for the rest of eternity.

It is amazing that you often pay the highest price for the lowest level of life, and yet in contrast, the highest level of life is a completely free gift from Jesus Christ. Never reduce your real world down to the size of the devil's world. He lives at the lowest level and we are called to live at the highest level.

IT IS A REDEFINING WORLD

This world of sickness and disease redefines who you are. When Andrew got sick with cancer, I went from being a leader of a growing church, to a parent whose son had a life threatening disease. I was being redefined by a world of sickness. All the new people in my life had no knowledge of my real world of ministry etc. but knew me as the father of a dying young man.

This made me mad. Why should I allow my life to be redefined by a sickness? Why should I allow such a change to

> *Start dreaming of the kind of world we believe God has created for us to live in.*

happen in my life? I know who I am. I do not have to live in the world of sickness nor does it have the right to redefine my life. This world has the ability to make you into an entirely different person, and I refused to let that happen. After Andrew died many people came up to us expecting to find us entirely different. Yes! There were some things that God had adjusted in our lives to make us better people, but we refused to let sickness and death redefine who we are.

We made up our mind that the world of sin, sickness, loss and death, would not become our world of reality. I purposed to live in a world created by God, full of abundance and blessing, with a hope of a great future. This is the world God has created for me and I choose to live in it by faith. When the enemy attempted to draw me into his world I deliberately decided that his world is not my reality and therefore I will not allow it to become my dominant world. We must make up our mind that the world of sickness, divorce, loss, death etc is not the world we must live in.

There are a few things we need to do to stay living in the real world of God's promises.

FIRST: Absolutely know that God lives in a world of peace and joy and blessing and that He wants us to enjoy the fullness of His world. Start dreaming of the kind of world we believe God has created for us to live in. We must not accept our present lot in life. There is hope for a better place and a greater day ahead. Believe that God has a great plan for our life and that we can fulfill it in this life.

SECOND: Make up our mind that whatever happens will never disqualify us from living in the love and blessing of God. Nothing we have done can negate God's love toward us. We can run often into the arms of our Father God and enjoy His love. More than anything else we must always remember that God loves us and will never give up on us. His plan and promises for us are still YES.

THIRD: Read the Bible and find God's promises that describe the kind of world you want to live in. It is there and it is available just for us. Confess His promises continually and create a world of confident expectation. We must stop regretting what has happened and stop talking about it. Get on with life and declare God's great promises.

FOURTH: Do not let defeated and negative people stop us from living in the real world of God's love and blessing. Do not let our broken world demand our unending allegiance. We may have to visit this world and even walk through it for a season, but it is not our dwelling place. Psalm 23 says that we are to walk through the valley of the shadow of death and not make it our resting place. Walk through the trial. Don't sit down and give up. We don't belong there and if we will keep getting up each morning and putting one foot in front of the other, we will eventually walk out of our dark valley. We do not have to do penance for our mistakes for the rest of our life once we have surrendered our failures to God.

> *We do not have to do penance for our mistakes for the rest of our life once we have surrendered our failures to God.*

FIFTH: Never let super-spiritual or religious people put yokes and burdens on us that God never intended us to carry. Jesus came to give us an abundant blessed life here on planet earth and with Him eternally. God created us for His pleasure, but He created earth for our pleasure. To impose awful routines and restrictions upon people because they are experiencing a season of "brokenness and failure" is to act like the Pharisees in the Bible whom Jesus rebuked. I was amazed that some people suggested we were enjoying life too much while we had a sick son. I just knew that God's love was toward us for good and all we needed to do was to live in His world of faith, hope and love.

By applying these five principles I found that I was able to live in a different world to the one that most people expected us to be in. Sure we had many challenges as we dealt with the madness of sickness and disease in our son Andrew, but we did not become prisoners in a world of hopelessness and failure.

Andrew's sickness has changed our lives, but thank God we have been redefined by God's grace and love, and the awesome promises of His word, and we have emerged from our valley of shadows as better people with a greater hope and a stronger confidence in the God we love to serve.

CHAPTER TWELVE

FACING THE FUNERAL

I watch as my children come and go
using our home as their base
Their security is found in our being there
And they never cease to need more resource in their unending
search for life
And I realise that my Father in heaven
feels the same way about me
And I hear Him say, you are my beloved son and I turn back
to Him and say,
You are my loving Father.

I see my children getting older
and disappearing into worlds of independence
And I wonder will I ever see them again
And yet they continue to return bringing with them
new found friends
And I realise that my Father in heaven has arranged
all these same things for me
And I hear Him say, you are my beloved son
and I turn back to him and say,
You are my loving Father

When sorrow comes into our lives and difficult times
make it hard to survive
In the turmoil of unexpected ends not hoped for or planned
And we group together drawing strength from our uniqueness
and our common bond
And I realise that my Father in heaven is not taken by
surprise by our lot
And I hear Him say, you are my beloved son and I turn back
to Him and say,
You are my loving Father

Steve Penny August 2003

I did not keep a diary for the last month of Andrew's sickness as we began to feel the impact of his declining health in a very real way. Andrew did not respond after the third round of Chemo and so the doctors finally told us that there was nothing more that they could do.

We then had to do the rounds of the people who could assist us with care when Andrew came home. We were told very vaguely that Andrew had less than six months to live. Most said that he would not see Christmas. Our lives were thrown again into turmoil as I had pinned everything on the promise that we would have a wonderful Christmas together with Andrew when he was healed. To now be told he would be dead before Christmas was tormenting beyond belief. We felt God had been given plenty of time to heal Andrew by now.

Andrew came home and began to deteriorate very quickly. He couldn't eat or drink and now could not even walk. The cancer had spread to areas where it had now cut off his ability to stand and was making it extremely difficult for him to pass urine. I had to lift Andrew as a dead weight out of his bed and hold him upright while he strained to pass urine into a bottle. It would take quite some time and I would be literally struggling to hold up this 90kg man. When he was finished we would both fall onto the bed exhausted.

I cannot even write about the last month with Andrew at home as it brings back so many deep memories of our son dying before our eyes. Marion and Anna were marvellous even during this time as they now had to bathe our big son and husband like a little baby. Words cannot describe what it is like to be a parent and watch your son waste away, with eyes that look at you knowing you are dying yet longing for a special miracle. Until the final Wednesday night, we never really talked about releasing Andrew to heaven. We staunchly continued on believing for that miracle, which we believed was our right.

It was on that Wednesday night as we laid the prayer cloth from church on Andrew's head that we decided to release our son into the arms of his Saviour. We just felt such a peace that God was in control and we knew that Andrew would soon be in heaven enjoying perfect health and strength forever. He was promoted peacefully into heaven the next morning.

The preparations for the funeral happened so quickly after the impact of Andrew's death that it seemed like we were acting out some role in a drama being played all around us. Our greatest memories of those days during the week between Andrew's passing and the funeral service were of the love we received from our friends worldwide.

It was a source of incredible joy to us to see florists lining up at the door with huge baskets of flowers. At times there were florists from various shops; their cars lined up in the driveway filled with many flower arrangements. We actually had to put a stop to the delivery of flowers as there was physically no more room in our house. We arranged to collect flowers in the weeks after the funeral, so that the love and well wishes kept coming for quite some time.

Our house literally became a "Garden of Eden" with every beautiful flower you could possibly imagine giving off its beautiful scent. Every area of our house was overrun with delightful beauty. No wonder the Bible declares that we can have "beauty for ashes." We now know what it means. Our house of mourning became a place of indescribable beauty.

It actually became a time of great release for us, as friends and family poured into our house to walk with us through our time of sorrow. The emails, faxes, cards and letters that streamed into our lives at this time became messages of healing from a loving heavenly Father using His family to bring healing to His children. The funeral itself was held in a Church in the Caloundra area, as we wanted it held local to where Andrew

> *Just because it is a sad day does not make it a bad day.*

had lived. It was wonderful to see so many of our neighbours and friends from the area attend the funeral, as did many of Andrew's surfing friends. The church was absolutely packed with standing room only and I was amazed to see so many of our ministry friends from all over Australia. We were very humbled by such a show of support. We will never forget such kindness to us. All our dear friends took part in the funeral and shared so lovingly on our behalf.

I wanted to preach at the funeral because I believed God had helped me to see that even though it was a sad day it was not a bad day in our lives. There was such a great sense of triumph in the place that I came out of the funeral service knowing that my Heavenly Father had all things under control. Even though I did not understand why Andrew was taken from us, I knew right there that God had a plan in it all and we would see the plan unfold as time went on. Something happened to me at the funeral that I cannot explain except that again I knew that God would turn our sorrow into other people's joy.

I want to share the key points of the message I gave at the funeral which was to me evidence of all that God had been doing in our lives over the past eight months. It was a declaration of triumph. Not false bravado or denial but absolute joy that we had come through the worst season of our lives as winners and over-comers because of the love of our Heavenly Father and His gift of faith in our lives.

As I stood to speak at Andrew's funeral I felt quite frail of physical stature as we were so wrung out from all that was happening, but I felt strong on the inside. God had perfected something in me that I knew would be seen in my life from this time on. I shared at the funeral how we had made some very important decisions about Andrew's death and burial.

WE CHOOSE TO MAKE TODAY A GOOD DAY.

Just because it is a sad day does not make it a bad day. The Bible says that all things work together for good and so we choose to make today a good day. If we make it a bad day, it will be filled with sorrow and loss and regrets. If we choose to make it a good day then we can fill it with hope for the future and believe that it will work out for our good.

We would never look on Andrew's death as an evil thing, but rather declare that even his funeral day is the day that the Lord has made.

WE CHOOSE TO ASK WHAT – NOT WHY?

We have made up our minds not to ask the kind of questions that have no answers this side of eternity. Asking why all the time only brings torment and prolongs the grief and sorrow. You may never really know why some things happen. The greatest question one can ever ask in any situation in life is, "what must I do to be saved?" We have made a choice to ask, what must we do to see God's plan of salvation happen for us in this present situation. We can then act in faith and go forward with positive hope for the future.

WE CHOOSE TO LOVE THE LIVING AND HONOUR THE DEAD.

We have decided to focus our attention on those who remain. Yes! We will honour and love the memories Andrew has left with us, but we will not sit at his shrine mourning his loss. We will make our remaining children, family and friends our highest priority and give ourselves to loving and enjoying them even more than before.

WE CHOOSE TO SOW A SEED NOT BURY A BODY.

We made the decision that Andrew's life would not be wasted and that we would sow his life as a seed which will bring many other sons into God's kingdom. We refused to bury a body and have some little plot in the ground as a place of remembrance. We chose to make Andrew's life and death an opportunity to reach others with the love of God. I believe for 1000 young men and women to be released into full time ministry over the next few years as the fruit of what God has done in our lives through this journey of faith with Andrew.

Since the funeral there have been many more challenges to face and memories to embrace. I miss Andrew so much and still look and listen for him. However the Lord gave me a promise that I would have the privilege of training up a thousand sons to serve in the ministry because I had stayed faithful to Him. I now look daily for those sons to emerge in my life and have already seen God give me sons in the ministry in many nations in the past months.

This book is not about the loss of a loved one – our son – nor about the tough road we have traveled. This book is about you. I have written it for every person who needs to run back to the love of God and find themselves again. This is about your life and the world God has for you. Whatever has entered your life, or whatever may have been taken from you, pales into insignificance when you realise what God has given to you in His son Jesus Christ. There is nothing to compare with the love of God and the sense of well being that comes when you hide yourself in His love. I pray that God Himself will become so real and powerful in your life that you will never doubt His love for you. I pray you will arise and stand up into all that Christ has for you, and believe in hope for a wonderful future. I pray that you will step out in faith relying on the Holy Spirit to empower you to do and achieve all that God has put in your heart to do. I pray that you will be abundantly blessed in all things and live an overcoming life bringing glory and honour to our Lord Jesus Christ.

May FAITH, HOPE AND LOVE be with you always!

For more information on resources from
Steve Penny Ministries

PO Box 650
Buderim QLD 4556
Australia

P: +61 7 5409 7009
E: spm@kings.org.au